Learning to Crew

Learning to Crew

Basil Mosenthal

ADLARD COLES NAUTICAL
London

Published 1998 by Adlard Coles Nautical
an imprint of A & C Black (Publishers) Ltd
35 Bedford Row, London WC1R 4JH

Copyright © Basil Mosenthal 1998

ISBN 0-7136-4970-4

A CIP catalogue record for this book is available from the
British Library.

Designed by Robert Mathias, Publishing Workshop

Typeset in 11/14pt Caslon by Robert Mathias, Publishing Workshop
Printed and bound in Singapore through Printlink International Co

Learning to Crew

This book is about crewing in 'live-aboard' boats, as opposed to dinghies. We will sometimes refer to them as 'yachts' and this may sound rather grand, but 'yacht' is a proper and useful description of a live-aboard boat of any size, sail or power, as opposed to a dinghy.

Opportunities to sail aboard these bigger boats certainly do exist, especially if you look for them. And skippers are happy to find enthusiastic crew members who are willing to learn and are 'good to have aboard'. In general we will be talking about boats that go cruising, because that is where most newcomers start. But there is nothing to stop you trying your hand at racing once you have gained some experience.

At the start you will learn most in a boat by watching the other crew. But a book can certainly help. It will give you an idea of what to expect when joining your first boat, help you find your way around on board, and explain what you'll need to learn first, such as a few basic seamanship skills. A book can also remind you of what not to do, because there are right and wrong ways of doing almost everything afloat. And if you learn the right way, not only will you be be a more useful crew, but you will also have more fun – and not worry that you may hurt yourself or that someone may shout at you.

Finally, you will note that both the skipper and the prospective crew are, in this book, referred to as 'he'. But it must be very clear that this is only for convenience, so for 'he' read 'he or she' throughout!

Contents

About this Book

This book is a simple introduction for anyone who has not crewed in a yacht before. It is not a complete crew's manual, but it concentrates on the essential matters because its clear aim is to get you started and have you joining in whatever is going on as soon as possible after you join your first yacht. If you glance through the Contents you will see how we will help you. We start by suggesting how to organise your arrival on board and what gear to bring.

There is then a guided tour of a typical boat, starting below decks, and including some remarks about life in a boat. Then, before you go to sea and start hoisting sails, you will need to find out the arrangements on deck. We point out the most important things (and names) to be learned first, and what remains will soon fall into place. Chapter 4 shows you some basic seamanship, such as how to handle lines properly and tie a few knots. This is routine stuff, but its important and it will help you join in on the boat

You will very soon discover that a lot happens on board that is not related to actually sailing the boat. For instance, she has to be made ready to go to sea, and when you return from a sail you will either need to anchor or else berth alongside. And all this very much involves the crew, as does being able to handle the dinghy. So there are chapters about all these aspects.

We have tried not to use unnecessary nautical jargon, but we have referred to parts of the boat by their proper nautical names, because a part of learning to crew is finding out what things on board are called. Generally the first time an important new word or expression is used it is put in italics.

Although this book starts from basics, we are assuming, as a new or prospective crew, that you will want to progress beyond just pulling on ropes – that you would eventually like to learn about everything in the boat, what its purpose is, and what is going on around you. For instance, we are assuming that you would like to know something about navigation and tides and generally understand what the skipper is trying to do when sailing the boat. You might even have an ambition to be a skipper yourself one day. So there are a couple of chapters on these subjects. But keep this in perspective. Don't get too enthusiastic about the GPS before you have learned how to coil a rope properly!

CHAPTER 1

New Crew

Correctly 'crew' is used to refer to everyone aboard. But it is also a convenient abbreviation for 'crew member'. So you will be to referred to as a 'new crew', which is less of a mouthful than 'new crew member'.

Making the arrangements

Arranging to join a boat may not be as simple as planning a game of tennis. So when you are in contact with the skipper, get all the details clear in advance. It will help you both.

☐ Agree the best time to come aboard and find out exactly where the boat will be berthed. The skipper may be planning to sail at a certain time, but you do not want to be leaping aboard the boat just as she is about to leave. If possible you need time to get your gear stowed, to find your way around the boat, and help to get her ready for sea. Sometimes you may be asked to come aboard in the evening ready for an early departure the next day.

☐ With a local weekend cruise there should be no problem in getting back in port on Sunday night. But on a passage or a longer cruise the weather can sometimes upset a schedule. So if you have a deadline for getting home; if it is essential to be back by Monday morning, then say so before you start. The skipper should be used to crew who have limited time available – provided they say so in advance.

It is reasonable to ask the skipper what his plans are. You might find that he wants to head off in a certain direction, depending, of course, on the weather. Or he may have a more relaxed view and say 'let's see what the weather looks like tomorrow, and decide then'. The cruising pattern for most boats is to sail during the day and settle themselves in harbour for the night. Depending on where you are, and on the skipper's preference, your nights may be spent at a marina or at anchor. But there may also be a night at sea. For instance many passages from the UK to mainland Europe or Ireland require a night at sea. If there is any chance of a foreign visit you will need your passport.

What gear to bring

Bringing the right gear aboard is not so much a question of how you look, as the important matter of keeping yourself dry, warm and comfortable, even in summer. Because if you are not warm and comfortable you will not enjoy yourself, and you will not be much use as a crew.

If you go dinghy sailing you may spend the afternoon afloat, and then retire to the clubhouse or go home and change into dry clothes. As we shall be reminding you, a live-aboard boat *is* your home – if only for a short while at a time.

Even on a sunny day, when the temperature ashore feels as if you should be in shorts and T-shirts, you will find that the breeze makes it much cooler on the water. You may need to put on extra clothing so be prepared. And although it may be summer, the nights can be much colder than you expect so take extra warm clothing, especially if you will be sailing at night.

If you don't own a set of 'thermals', take a couple of sweaters, and remember that several thin layers are warmer than one thick one. Some kind of hat or cap will also help keep you warm.

Then there is the question of keeping dry. It may be a beautiful day, but if you are sailing fast you can easily get spray aboard. There may be rainy days or even rough weather. Being wet means soon getting cold, so the idea is to try not to get wet in the first place. You really need waterproof gear that is designed for sailing, and this is usually called 'foul weather gear' or 'oilskins' ('oilies'). The other

benefit of waterproof gear is that it also keeps the wind out, so it will help to keep you warm.

Modern waterproof gear for boats can be highly efficient, but it can also be very expensive. There are cheaper versions, although they may not be so effective or hard-wearing. So if you don't have any waterproof gear, try borrowing, scrounging, or even hiring something waterproof. If you ask the skipper he may have a spare set aboard.

But don't just arrive on board hoping for the best.

▼ A good suit of oilskins not only keeps you dry, but will keep you warm as well. Gloves are a matter of personal preference, but if you do wear them they should be proper sailing gloves. Ordinary gloves can get caught up in winches.

Water gets in not so much by penetrating the fabric of foul weather gear, as through the various necessary openings such as up the sleeves or round the neck. A towel or strip of towelling worn round the neck as a scarf is a good idea, and if there are no inside cuffs on your sleeves, a couple of strong elastic bands can help. Trousers that fit high up on the chest are the best. One-piece suits work well, although not everyone likes them.

☐ Shoes with proper non-skid soles are essential; any other type can be positively dangerous. Canvas shoes can do perfectly well – provided they have the right soles. Be warned that trainers do not give a grip on wet decks unless they are specially designed for boats.

For the other garments, it's up to you. But you do need at least one change of the clothes you will wear at sea, as well as dry clothes to wear ashore – more if you will be on board for any length of time.

▼ A detail of a built-in harness attachment on a foul weather jacket. The safety line is simply and easily clipped to the metal ring attached to the strengthened waistband of the jacket.

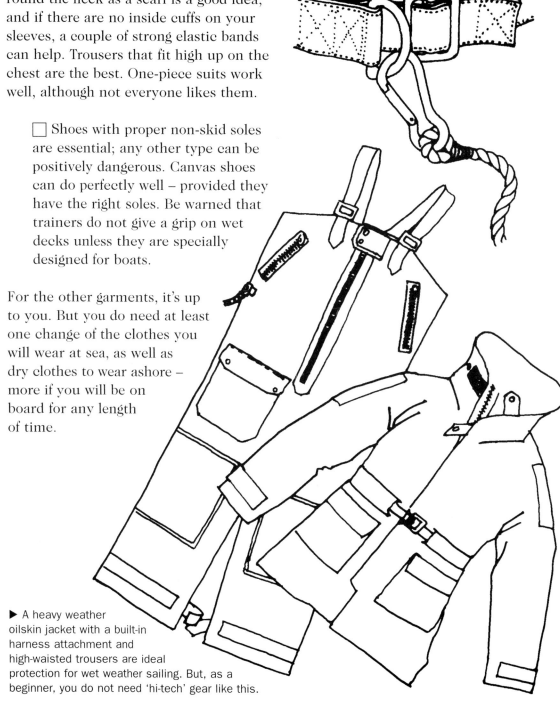

▶ A heavy weather oilskin jacket with a built-in harness attachment and high-waisted trousers are ideal protection for wet weather sailing. But, as a beginner, you do not need 'hi-tech' gear like this.

Other items of gear

In addition to your clothing, here is a list of the things you are likely to find useful.

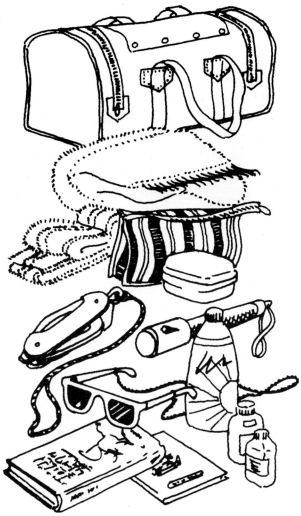

Towel – *full size*
A small towel – *to use as a neck scarf inside your foul weather gear when the weather is bad*
Toilet gear
Soap – *in a handy plastic box for showers ashore*
A pocket knife – *that is always carried with you on board*
Pocket flashlight
Sun glasses – *have them on a string in case they get knocked off*
Sun screen – *you will get sunburnt much more easily on the water than on the shore*
Sea sickness remedy (*see below*)
Something to read
Medication – *bring any that you take regularly, or might need to take*
Passport – *if there is a chance of a foreign visit*

Note: If you suffer from asthma, or any other chronic ailment, you should tell the skipper, even though this does not incapacitate you in any way. You should have all the medication you need with you.

☐ A small zip bag is handy for keeping small personal things together, along with your wallet and camera.

> VERY LIKELY YOU WILL BE ASKED TO BRING YOUR OWN SLEEPING BAG, ALTHOUGH A FEW BOATS DO HAVE THEIR OWN. YOU MUST CHECK ON THIS.

Space aboard is always limited, so don't bring unnecessary gear. But do bring enough. It is annoying for the rest of the crew if you obviously haven't enough clothing to keep yourself warm and they feel they have to lend you theirs. You can always ask for advice about what to bring, and it can be an education to see what an experienced sailor unpacks from their bag.

Bring your gear in a bag that will stow easily. A knapsack may be OK provided it does not have a rigid frame, but a long soft bag is the best.

Although warmth and comfort are certainly the most important considerations when packing clothing, you may not be able to forget entirely about how you look. When you go sailing you become a part of the crew of that particular boat while you are on board, and it may not be appreciated if you go ashore looking too scruffy.

Money

The arrangements vary between boats, and it saves embarrassment to ask early on. Sometimes the skipper acts as host and treats his crew as guests. But it is common for at least the cost of food to be shared, and there are other expenses such as fuel and mooring fees to be considered. Younger crew members are usually not asked to pay a share – unless all the crew are young. If you do not have to contribute in cash, it is a nice gesture to bring along some kind of food or drink to share.

▲ It is quite common for the crew to contribute to the running expenses of a yacht; helping to pay for the fuel, for example.

Seasickness

Don't be put off by this subject so early in the book. It is best to be quite open about it and get it out of the way. Almost everyone who goes to sea has been seasick at some time, but most get over it and it is nothing whatever to be ashamed of.

In fact boats don't go looking for rough weather, and the chances are that most of your sailing will be in calm water, but it cannot be guaranteed. So let's see if anything can be done to keep this problem under control.

If you have not been sailing before, you may not really know whether you are liable to be seasick or not. A trip on a large car ferry will not be a proper test. But if the skipper suggests that you might have a bumpy ride it is wise to take some sensible precautions, at least the first time – then you can see how things work out.

There are a few well-worn rules that make sense when it comes to seasickness, but they are often ignored:

☐ There are several advertised remedies, ranging from pills to wrist bands to patches that go behind the ear. Not all seasickness remedies work for everyone, but give them a trial and there will probably be one that works for you if you need it.

☐ Seasickness remedies should be taken *in advance* – it is usually too late when you are already feeling sick.

☐ Being cold (and wet) certainly increases the risk of feeling sick. Go below and get properly dressed *before you feel too ill to go below!* Better still, come up on deck properly dressed to start with – and this applies whether you are seasick or not.

☐ It is always said that if you keep busy (for instance by steering) you will have less time to worry about being sick, and that if you are feeling ill it helps to keep looking at the horizon.

☐ Watch what you eat – and drink. A heavy night at the pub may not be the best preparation for a choppy sea the next day, nor would a big fry-up for breakfast; try porridge if it is available. Oxo, Bovril or soup may be better than tea or coffee, and beware of orange juice. Fizzy drinks help, and toast or dry biscuits are always safe. But everyone has their own ideas. If you think you might be ill, don't worry about it, just be careful about what you eat and drink for the first couple of days. Then you will forget about it.

▲ There is much more chance of you feeling ill If you are cold, so dress up warm before you go on deck.

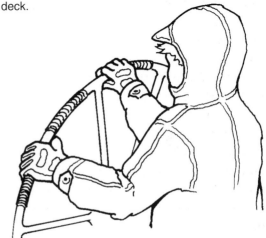

▲ Taking a turn at the helm will take your mind of feeling seasick.

▲ A good hot drink will not only keep you warm but will also help to keep seasickness at bay.

▲ If you start to feel ill, watch the horizon and look out for the next navigation point on your trip.

CHAPTER 2

Staying Aboard

The biggest difference between crewing in a cruising yacht and sailing a dinghy is that you will be _staying aboard_. There are things to be learnt about living aboard a boat as opposed to going for a day's sail.

So assuming that you have arrived on board with your gear, let's start off by looking around below decks. There are differences in the way boats are laid out down below as well as on deck, partly depending on the size of the boat. But the general features are much the same in all boats.

Typically there is a cabin up forward with two bunks or a double bunk, then there may be a toilet compartment on one side and a wardrobe opposite. In larger boats there may be a shower in the toilet compartment.

In the main cabin there will be settees on each side, which are used for sitting by day and as bunks by night. There will be stowage behind the back cushions of the settees (often used for bedding), more lockers under the settee cushions, and lockers or shelves above. There will be a table, which may fold up completely or have drop leaves.

Food is prepared and cooked in the _galley_ at the after end of the cabin, with the navigator's chart table on the opposite side. Steps will lead up to the _companion way_, the hatch which leads out on deck and into the _cockpit_. The engine is usually under this ladder and boxed in.

Further aft again there may be another berth, which is known as a _quarter berth_ because this part of a vessel is known as her quarters. In some larger yachts it is common for there to be another complete _after cabin_.

DIRECTIONS

Sailors talk about below and on deck eg 'I am going below as it is cold on deck'. 'Upstairs' and 'downstairs' are never used in a boat, and for some reason sailors find it extremely funny if anyone uses either of these words .

PORT QUARTER — PORT SIDE — PORT BOW — STERN — ◀ AFT — BEAM — AMIDSHIPS — FORE ▶ — BOW — STARBOARD QUARTER — STARBOARD SIDE — STARBOARD BOW

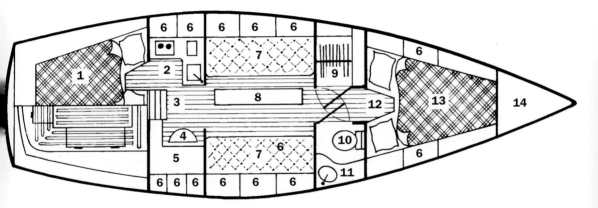

▲ PLAN SHOWING THE LAYOUT OF A TYPICAL 30FT YACHT

1. Stern cabin
2. Galley
3. Companionway steps
4. Navigator's seat
5. Navigation table
6. Storage lockers
7. Saloon berth/settee
8. Fold-down saloon table
9. Wardrobe
10. WC
11. Wash basin
12. Fore cabin
13. Double berth
14. Chain locker

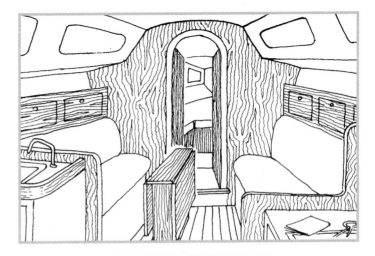

▲ A TYPICAL VIEW OF THE MAIN SALOON

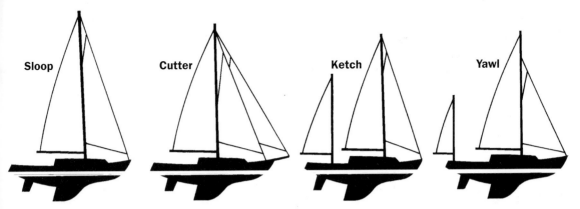

Sloop   Cutter   Ketch   Yawl

These days the most popular type of boat is a sloop, with a mainsail set aft of the single mast and a single headsail set ahead of the mast. This will be the type of boat we are going to talk about throughout this book, but you will not find any problems if you are sailing in another type of boat such as a cutter which has two headsails, a ketch which has a main mast and a mizzen mast (aft), or a yawl, which has two masts like a ketch, but the aft mast is set behind the rudder post.

Storage

There is always a lot of equipment to stow away in any boat – the boat's equipment, the food provisions and the crew's personal gear and bedding. You will find there are (or should be) plenty of lockers and drawers everywhere for this and the best use has to be made of every bit of storage space.

☐ *'A place for everything and everything in its place'* can be a boring idea, because many of us are not naturally tidy. But it is essential in a boat. For instance emergency gear such as life-jackets or the medical kit may be needed in a hurry and they must always be in a particular place so that everyone knows where they are.

☐ But there are other items to consider. For example, the pencil for the log book, a screwdriver, or the tea bags may not be needed as an emergency, but it can be extremely annoying for everyone if they are not where they should be.

So try to find out where everything is stowed, and then, whatever you use, *put it back where it belongs.*

Secure at sea

Any sailing boat can heel over, even in light winds, and on a calm day the wash from another passing vessel can make it rock around. So when a boat is at sea, everything below must always be secure.

You will see that all lockers and drawers have positive catches so that they cannot fly open, and these must always be properly shut. Doors should either be fully shut, or latched in the open position. When you are sitting in the cockpit at sea, you will discover that one of the most unwelcome sounds is a banging door below or – even worse – the crash as something that has not been properly stowed falls out.

You will also see low vertical strips round the edge of the table, the galley working surfaces, and shelves. These are known as *fiddles,* and they are intended to prevent things sliding off the table surfaces when the boat heels.

▲ A fiddle will prevent flat objects, such as plates, sliding off the table, but make sure bottles are well stowed before putting to sea.

▲ Some drawers are designed to be lifted before they are opened. This device stops them sliding out when the boat is heeled.

◄ Good steady bottle storage is essential when at sea.

Stowing your gear

You should be allocated a locker for your
gear and possibly a drawer for the smaller
items. Anything that will not go in the
locker will have to stay in your bag,
which will be stowed away somewhere
secure. If in doubt, ask where. In some
boats there are small lockers in the toilet
compartment for individual toilet gear.

At first you may find it hard living with
so much less room for your things. But
with all the crew living in a small space,
untidiness just does not work, and you
will soon learn to get yourself organised.

☐ If you are sleeping in a berth in the
main cabin, you will need to roll up
your sleeping bag in the morning and
stow it away (ask where) to leave the
cabin clear for breakfast.

Except in a very small boat, there will
usually be a locker specifically reserved
for foul weather gear. If you come down
from the deck in wet gear, always take it
off at the bottom of the companionway
steps and stow it in the wet locker before
making the rest of the cabin wet.

Fresh water

You may have to pump water to the tap,
although many boats now have a pressure
water system.

☐ The supply of fresh water is limited
by the amount that the boat can carry
in its tanks. Remember this when you
wash up, clean your teeth or think
about having a shower – *never leave a
tap running!*

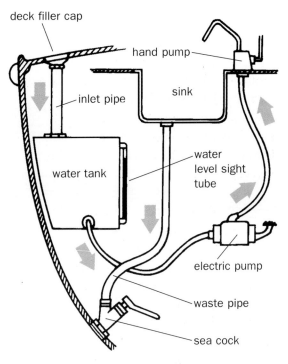

▲ A typical fresh water supply system.

A well organised crew will cook and eat
quite happily, but still end up with the
minimum of dirty dishes to be washed.
And you will learn to keep yourself shaven
and wholesome without anything like the
amount of water you use ashore.

The skipper will know when fresh
water will next be available – whether
the present supply will have to last for
three or four more days, or if water will
be available tomorrow. It is easy to fill up
with fresh water at a marina, sometimes
difficult elsewhere. A couple of jerrycans
may be kept on board to take ashore for
filling as a back-up fresh water supply.

Some boats have a sea water tap in the
galley as well the fresh water supply.
There are some jobs such as washing up
that can, at a pinch, be done with sea
water and plenty of detergent, and this
does save the fresh water supply.

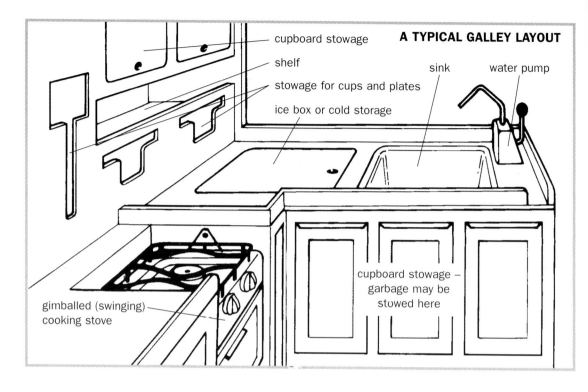

A TYPICAL GALLEY LAYOUT

cupboard stowage

shelf

sink

water pump

stowage for cups and plates

ice box or cold storage

cupboard stowage – garbage may be stowed here

gimballed (swinging) cooking stove

The galley

The galley will have a sink, and there will be fixed racks for mugs and plates as well as the most frequently used items. As usual in a boat, a lot has to be fitted into a small space, and it has to be secure.

Cooking is most likely to be done with gas, and there will be a stove with the gas supplied from a cylinder stowed in a separate locker on deck.

☐ Cooking gas is perfectly safe if it is used properly, but highly dangerous if not. The gas is heavy and will lurk in the bottom of the boat if it does leak. You will be warned (or you should be) about making sure that the taps on the stove are always turned off when the burners are not in use, and the gas should be turned off *at the cylinder* when cooking is finished.

☐ Cooking gas has a distinctive and unpleasant smell. Always say if you think you can smell it and never light the stove (or a cigarette) if there is the slightest smell of gas Many boats have gas detectors and alarms.

You must learn to use the stove safely, even if you hesitate to offer your services as a cook, because everyone aboard should at least be able to brew up a hot drink. Incidentally, great care needs to be used in the galley at sea. If the boat moves unexpectedly it is easy for the cook to pour hot liquid over himself while filling a mug. In choppy weather it is always recommended that the cook wears foul weather trousers.

Galley stoves are usually pivoted on swinging gymbals so that they remain horizontal when the boats heels over. However, when you are in harbour it is safer to lock the stove in one position.

Meals on board will vary according to the weather. Typically the crew will eat breakfast down below, but lunch and tea may be picnic style in the cockpit as the boat will often be sailing. Supper will again tend to be in the cabin. And in most boats there are plenty of snacks in between. There will be a rubbish bin somewhere in the galley area and *all* waste material should go in it – *nothing* should be thrown overboard.

The toilet (*usually called the 'heads'*)

Let's not be prudish about this, because misunderstandings here can cause problems. First of all you must find out how to operate the toilet. There are various types of marine toilet, but essentially they all work by pumping sea water in to flush the toilet and then pumping it out again.

You will need to know the pumping procedure and there are often written instructions, but if in the slightest doubt – just ask. There may be valves (*sea-cocks*) to open and close. There will be one pipe where the sea water is pumped in, and another one where it is pumped out again. Sometimes these are closed after each time the toilet is used, and sometimes they are only closed when the crew finally leave the yacht. It is important to get it right, as sometimes failing to close a seacock can risk flooding. All this may sound complicated, but it is really very simple in practice.

The 'electrics'

You also need be careful about using the lights on board, as well as watching the fresh water, because the supply of electricity is limited. So lights should not be turned on when they are not needed.

The boat's electrical system will normally be supplied by two 12 volt batteries. One of these is kept for starting the engine (which is the most important thing that a battery has to do), and the other is used for 'services', which means the lighting and all the electronics. In many boats there may be an increasing number of items (e g a small hi-fi system!) that need battery power, which is why care is needed.

The batteries are charged by the engine when it is running, and if you are spending the day in harbour, the skipper may decide to run the engine for half an hour or so to top up the batteries.

'NOTHING THAT YOU HAVE NOT EATEN'

IN MANY BOATS YOU WILL FIND A NOTICE WARNING YOU ABOUT PUTTING THE WRONG THINGS DOWN THE HEADS – IT MAY BE SOMETHING LIKE '*NOTHING THAT YOU HAVE NOT ALREADY EATEN*'. THE HARD FACT IS THAT MARINE TOILETS DO GET BLOCKED FAR MORE EASILY THAN SHORESIDE TOILETS.

UNBLOCKING OFTEN MEANS DISMANTLING THE TOILET AND THIS IS NOT THE MOST PLEASANT JOB. IT USUALLY FALLS TO THE POOR SKIPPER (WHO WILL BE THE ONLY PERSON WHO KNOWS HOW TO DO IT) SO HE WILL UNDOUBTEDLY HAVE STRONG VIEWS ON THE SUBJECT!

The chart table

Except in the smallest boats, there will be a *chart table* where at least a folded chart can be laid out and the skipper (or whoever is doing the navigating) can do his work.

Spare charts are stowed inside the chart table, and there will be a bookcase for the navigational books. The VHF radio and any other electronic gear will be sited nearby. As well as being a flat space to lay out the chart, a chart table also becomes a convenient spot to put things down. But the navigator will not appreciate it if your book or sun glasses are sitting just where he wants to start plotting a course. And if the skipper chooses to leave a coffee mug stain on his expensive chart – well, that is up to him, but it is not recommended for the crew!

Housekeeping

There is less housekeeping to be done on a boat than at home, but meals still have to be prepared and the dirty dishes and pans washed up afterwards. The galley has to be kept clean and tidy (work surfaces, where the crew's food is prepared, should always be spotless) as does the toilet compartment, and the cabin deck (the *cabin sole*) needs a regular sweep and wipe over. None of this takes very long, but the whole crew are expected to do their share.

It is not suggested that the new crew should become a 'galley slave', but when he may not have many other skills to offer, he can make a good impression by being willing to do at least a full share of the domestic chores.

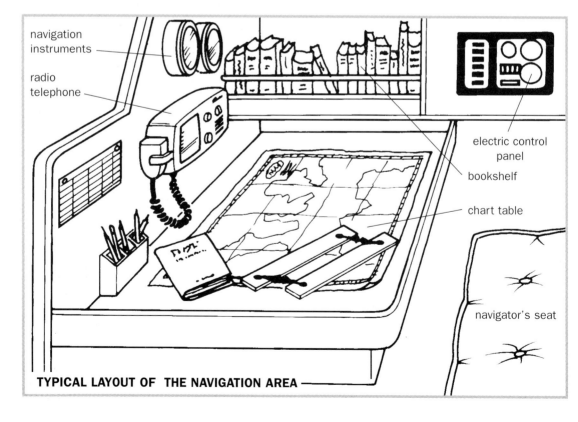

navigation instruments

radio telephone

electric control panel

bookshelf

chart table

navigator's seat

TYPICAL LAYOUT OF THE NAVIGATION AREA

Safety equipment – harnesses and lifejackets

Safety will be mentioned in various places in this book. Sailing is a very safe sport, and it remains so only by the crew taking sensible precautions against possible hazards such as fire, or falling overboard. In the unlikely event of something going wrong, not only must the right safety equipment need to be on board but the crew must also know where it is stowed and how to use it.

The skipper has a responsibility to make sure that the crew know about this, but some discretion is exercised. He will hardly want to welcome his new crew by immediately showing them how to launch the liferaft. Equally, a new arrival may find it embarrassing to ask where his life-jacket is stowed as soon as he steps aboard.

In practice the skipper may feel that a full briefing on safety equipment (which includes the fire extinguishers, medical kit, flares, and liferaft) is not necessary for a local sail in good weather, although he will probably tell you where the life-jackets are stowed. But for a longer time afloat he should give you a more detailed briefing. He may point out how to operate the radio in an emergency situation. The crew will need to know how to do this should the skipper get sick or be injured.

Safety harnesses are important because they are not just for use in an emergency, they should be worn on deck even in moderately bad weather and always at night. They need adjusting to fit each individual, so a harness will be allocated to each member of the crew. Try yours on, adjust it to fit (get help if necessary), then stow it with the rest of your kit.

TYPICAL SAFETY EQUIPMENT

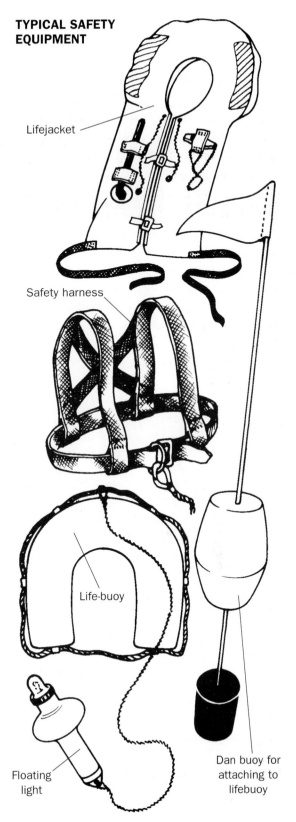

Lifejacket

Safety harness

Life-buoy

Floating light

Dan buoy for attaching to lifebuoy

CHAPTER 3

On Deck

While you are still in harbour, take the chance to look around on deck so that you can start finding out what things are called and how they are used before you begin sailing.

Nautical terms

As soon as you become involved with boats and the sea, you'll come across lots of new words and expressions like galley, heads and companion way. It may sometimes seem that sailors enjoy having a language of their own, but almost everything aboard a ship or boat is different from anything ashore, so it has its own special name.

If you have sailed in a dinghy, some items will be familiar to you because they are basically the same in a yacht as they are in a dinghy – just bigger. If you have not sailed before, there will be new words to learn.

Around the deck

There are very many different yacht designs, but the deck layout is essentially the same on all of them. If you can find your way around one boat, you will have no problem with others.

☐ What you see on deck, and what it is used for, is more easily explained by illustrations, and the one opposite shows everything that you need to make a start. Take time to note all these and you will find that other things soon fall into place.

Now look around the deck – or at the drawing – and note these key points:

☐ The mast is supported by wire *shrouds* on either side, by a *forestay* leading to the bow, and a *backstay* leading to the stern.

☐ Of the various ropes that you see, the two most important are the *halyards* which hoist the sails, and the *sheets* which control the sails once they are hoisted. So there is a *jib halyard* and a *main halyard*, *jib sheets* and the *main sheet*.

☐ The *main sheet*, which controls the mainsail, consists of a pair of blocks. The upper block is secured to the boom. and the lower one to the deck, usually to a fitting in a track so that it can slide across the boat. You will be using the mainsheet constantly, so look at the mainsheet in your boat and make sure you know how it works.

☐ The *topping lift* is the line leading from the the outer end of the main boom up to the masthead, and then down the mast to where it is tied on to a cleat. The topping lift supports the boom when the mainsail is not hoisted. Find out where it is secured

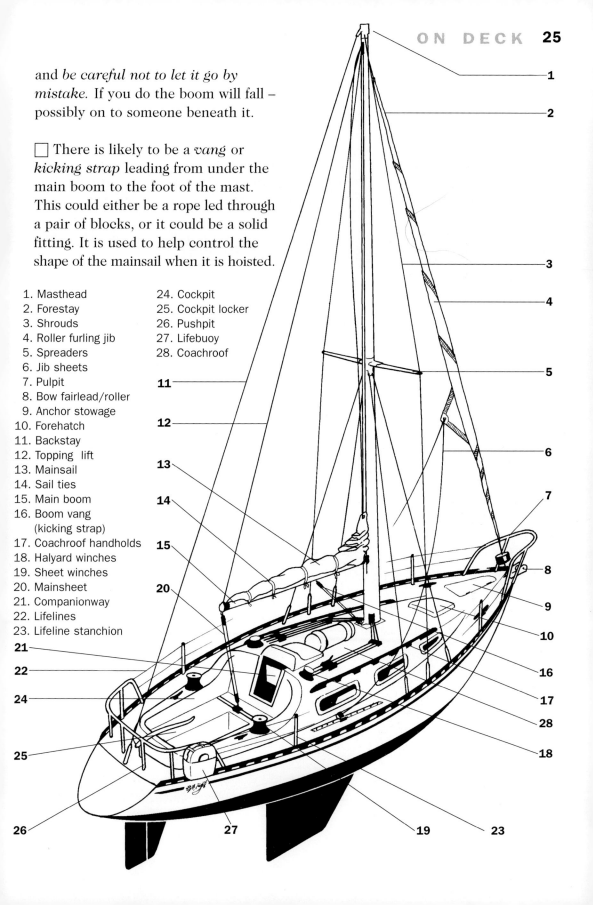

and *be careful not to let it go by mistake.* If you do the boom will fall – possibly on to someone beneath it.

☐ There is likely to be a *vang* or *kicking strap* leading from under the main boom to the foot of the mast. This could either be a rope led through a pair of blocks, or it could be a solid fitting. It is used to help control the shape of the mainsail when it is hoisted.

1. Masthead
2. Forestay
3. Shrouds
4. Roller furling jib
5. Spreaders
6. Jib sheets
7. Pulpit
8. Bow fairlead/roller
9. Anchor stowage
10. Forehatch
11. Backstay
12. Topping lift
13. Mainsail
14. Sail ties
15. Main boom
16. Boom vang
   (kicking strap)
17. Coachroof handholds
18. Halyard winches
19. Sheet winches
20. Mainsheet
21. Companionway
22. Lifelines
23. Lifeline stanchion
24. Cockpit
25. Cockpit locker
26. Pushpit
27. Lifebuoy
28. Coachroof

The cockpit

This is where the crew sit on deck when at sea, from where the boat is steered from and where the sheets are handled. In fact, it is the control centre of the boat, as it is in an aircraft.

One basic difference between boats is that some (mostly the smaller ones) are steered by a tiller while larger boats use wheel steering.

The *steering compass* is sited where it can be easily seen by the helmsman, and the engine controls are close at hand. You may also see a display for the *echo sounder* which shows the depth under the boat (important when in shallow water or finding a spot to anchor) and for the speedometer. Incidentally, leaving your camera, your Walkman or any other electronic or metal object near the compass can upset it and make it give a false reading.

There should be either one or two horseshoe lifebuoys mounted on the lifelines within reach of the helmsman. These are for throwing over immediately in the event of someone falling overboard.

Any water that gets into the cockpit will drain overboard through drains in the cockpit floor. Underneath one of the seats there will usually be a deep locker where buckets, fenders, mooring lines, and other deck gear can be stowed. This locker should be kept closed and fastened at sea.

The foredeck

In the bows the lifelines are secured to an arrangement of metal rails which go round the bow to protect anyone working up forward. This is the *pulpit* – not a hard term to remember.

The anchor is either stowed inside a hatch on the foredeck or lashed on deck.

▶ **TYPICAL COCKPIT LAYOUT**

1. Lifebuoy
2. Mooring cleat
3. Pushpit
4. Liferaft
5. Dan buoy
6. Helmsman's seat
7. Steering wheel
8. Compass binnacle
9. Sheet cleat
10. Cockpit sole
11. Cockpit locker
12. Sheet winch
13. Mainsheet traveller
14. Instruments
15. Companionway
16. Genoa track

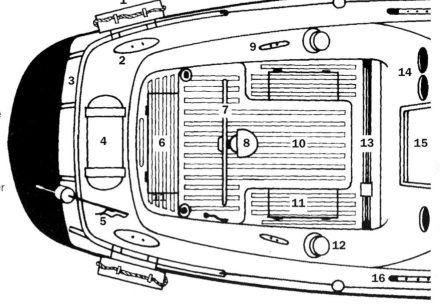

TYPICAL FOREDECK LAYOUT

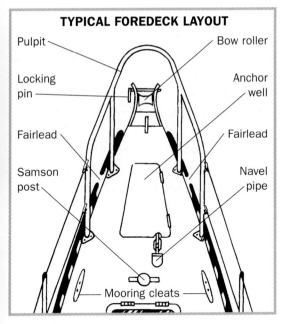

Pulpit

Bow roller

Locking pin

Anchor well

Fairlead

Fairlead

Samson post

Navel pipe

Mooring cleats

PARTS OF A SAIL

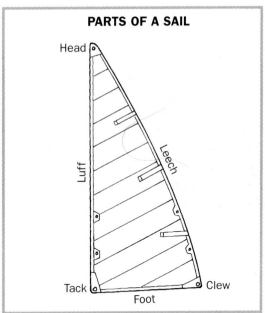

Head

Luff

Leech

Tack

Clew

Foot

Right in the bow is a roller where the chain is led when the boat is anchored.

On either side of the foredeck there are *cleats*, used for securing mooring lines when the boat is lying alongside a pontoon, and possibly a *samson post* for securing the anchor cable when she is at anchor.

> ANY SAIL SET FORWARD OF THE MAST IS CALLED A **HEADSAIL**. A SMALLER HEADSAIL IS REFERRED TO AS A **JIB**, AND A BIGGER HEADSAIL IS A **GENOA**. YOU MAY HEAR ANY OF THESE TERMS USED IN YOUR BOAT.

Winches, and using them

Deck fittings on boat are known as *hardware* and some of the most important pieces of hardware on a sailing boat are her *winches*. You must learn how to use a winch, and there is more about this in Chapter 6. Meanwhile have a look at the winches themselves.

A winch is a metal drum with an internal ratchet that allows it to rotate in one direction only, it has an opening on the top where a handle can be inserted in order to turn it.

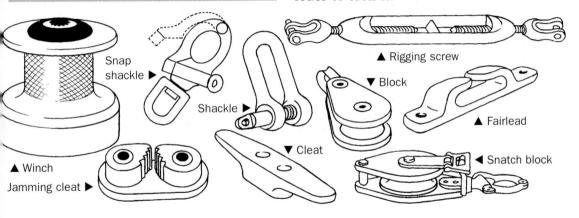

Snap shackle ▶

▲ Rigging screw

▼ Block

Shackle ▶

▲ Fairlead

▼ Cleat

▲ Winch

Jamming cleat ▶

◀ Snatch block

Winches are used in two ways. Because they will only turn in one direction, a rope can be wrapped round them to resist a strong pull (the more turns there are the greater the resistance).

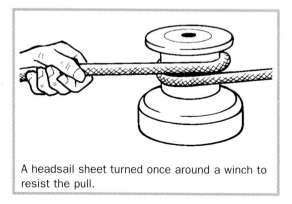

A headsail sheet turned once around a winch to resist the pull.

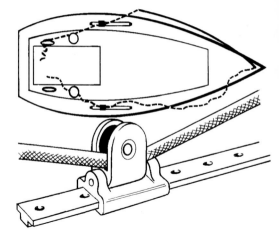

▲ A typical layout showing the arrangement of the genoa sheets led back from the foredeck, through the sheet lead, and into the cockpit.

Or the handle can be inserted in the top to wind in the rope.

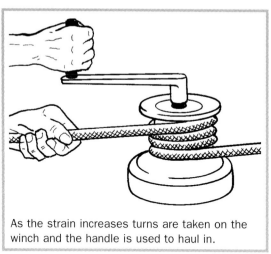

As the strain increases turns are taken on the winch and the handle is used to haul in.

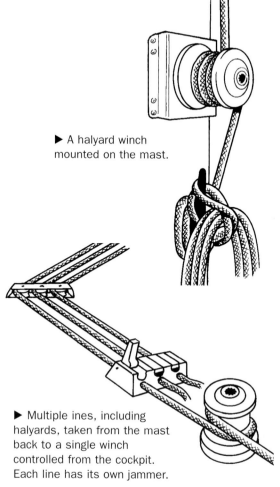

▶ A halyard winch mounted on the mast.

Winches are used for two purposes:

☐ as *sheet winches* to control and haul in the sheets, (the lines that control the sails).

☐ as *halyard winches* for hoisting the sails

▶ Multiple ines, including halyards, taken from the mast back to a single winch controlled from the cockpit. Each line has its own jammer.

Moving around safely

A yacht's deck has few clear spaces and it is covered with a great many obstacles. At sea it is rarely quite still (pitching and rolling with the motion of the waves) and may often be heeled over at an angle for long periods of time, so get used to moving about on a slant. This is why non-skid soles for your shoes are essential, and any other type is dangerous.

In hot weather bare feet do provide a good grip, but it is easy to stub a toe painfully on a deck fitting and they are not recommended. Many skippers object to them.

☐ The deck is not a place for rushing, but there is no need to be dead slow either. You'll get into the habit of moving around quickly enough, but take care and watch how you go.

There is an old sailor's expression *'One hand for the ship, and one for yourself'*, which means whatever the job you are doing, don't forget to hang on as well. There are plenty of things to hang on to: for instance there will be a grab-rail along the top of the *coachroof* on either side, and if you are moving along the deck the shrouds provide a good firm handhold. But try not to hold on to a rope line such as the mainsheet, because someone might be just about to release it.

There are wire *lifelines*, supported at intervals by *stanchions* all round the deck. At the bow they join the pulpit, which you have already noted, and at the stern there is a similar arrangement, officially called the *stern pulpit*, but almost always known as the *pushpit*.

When climbing aboard from a dinghy or the dock, use the stanchions to support yourself rather than the lines themselves, but try to hold on to the foot of the stanchion rather than the top – it puts less strain on it. It is better to hold on to the shrouds if they are near at hand.

We have already talked about safety harnesses. They must be worn on deck at night, and in choppy conditions. The skipper is likely to say when they must be worn, but you may certainly wear one at any time if it helps you move around the deck more confidently. It is not sissy to wear a harness, it is good sense.

☐ But a harness is useless if the lanyard is not clipped to the boat (i.e. if you are not *'clipped on'*). Learn how to move around easily while wearing a harness, and the best places to clip on. Most boats have a continuous line (a *jackstay*) for clipping on a harness which leads from the cockpit to the bows on each side of the boat. At night and in bumpy weather, when you are coming up from below, it is best to clip yourself on while you are still in the companion way. Then sort yourself out when you are safely in the cockpit.

LIFELINES ARE THERE TO KEEP YOU INBOARD, AND THEY ARE MORE THAN STRONG ENOUGH TO SUPPORT YOUR WEIGHT. BUT **NEVER** SIT ON THEM, EITHER AT SEA OR IN HARBOUR. APART FROM PUTTING UNNECESSARY STRAIN ON THEM, IT IS TOO EASY TO GET PITCHED BACKWARDS INTO THE WATER.

CHAPTER 4

Ropes & Knots

'Rope' is the most useful word for the heading of this chapter because everyone knows what it means. In fact, the ropes that you find in dinghies and yachts are almost always called *lines*.

Rope, or whatever you choose to call it, has been in use at sea in some form for as long as there have been sailors. It will always be an essential part of seagoing, whether it is used for a dinghy main sheet or the huge hawsers that secure super-tankers alongside a dock.

☐ Handling lines, whether they be sheets, halyards, or mooring lines, is a simple, basic, but essential crew skill. It comes into almost everything that happens on deck So we need to look at this subject straight away.

Types of rope

There are two main types of rope:

3-strand – This is also sometimes called laid rope because, when it is made, threads are twisted into strands which are laid up to form the rope.

Braided – In this type of cordage there is a core of fibres surrounded by a braided sheath. This rope is rather less likely to kink than 3-strand rope, but generally both types are handled in the same way.

Ropes are now made in a variety of colours which are increasingly used to 'colour-code' the various lines in a boat. So in your early days you might even be told 'the topping lift is the 'blue one'.

Coiling lines

A line that is not in use should be coiled up. This applies to a spare line such as a mooring line that is coiled up before it is stowed away, and also to halyards that have one end secured.

Lines lying around in a tangle look sloppy and they can get in the way. The important thing when they are coiled is that you can easily see the end, they are easier to stow, and are ready for use when needed again

Lines are coiled *clockwise*, using one hand for the coiling and holding the made-up coils in the other. If one end of the line is secured, you start at that end and work towards the loose end.

To coil a line neatly *you must try to get the kinks out of it*, particularly with 3-strand rope. With a little practice, a few kinks can be flicked as you make up the coil. But if the line is badly kinked it is better to stretch it out and untwist it before you begin to coil it.

TIDYING UP A LINE

Making up a line ▼ After a line (e g
a mooring line) is coiled, it can be
made up for stowage like this. This
allows it to be stowed easily and
tidily, ready for when it is needed
again.

◄ A sloppy
uncoiled line.

Cleats

You will see *cleats* in several places round
the deck. They are used for *turning up*
the ends of lines – both the lines used for
securing the boat to a dock and the lines
used for hoisting and controlling the sails.
You must know how to turn up a line on
a cleat correctly.

If the line is not going to be needed in
a hurry, or when it needs to be extra
secure (for instance a mooring line) the
last turn can be a jamming turn. But a
jamming turn is never used on any line
which may have to be released quickly,
such as a sheet.

An anchor chain is usually secured to a
samson post on the bow just like a rope.

TURNING UP A LINE ON A CLEAT

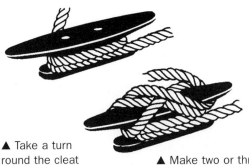

▲ Take a turn
round the cleat
(usually clockwise).

▲ Make two or three
figure-of-eight turns.

▲ Finish off with
another round turn.

▲ Make the last turn a
jamming turn.

Catch a turn!

'Catching a turn' is another simple but essential skill. If you are holding on to a line, there is a limit to the direct pull that you can resist. But if you *catch a turn* smartly round a cleat, a post, or a winch (and you usually have to be quick about it), you can withstand a much greater pull and keep things under control. Be prepared to catch a turn at any time you are handling a line – it could be a sheet, a mooring line, or the anchor line.

Throwing a line

This is most often needed to pass a mooring line to the shore when you are coming alongside. There are times, for instance when the skipper is trying to berth the boat alongside on a windy day, when it is important that the first throw is successful. But you also might have to throw a line to a person in the water, or

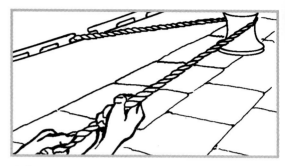
▲ Catching a turn to control the pull on a line.

to a dinghy needing help. So it is a simple skill that you should learn.

If you watch someone make a mess of throwing a line (and they often do) it is almost always because the line was not properly coiled to start with.

In an emergency a line might have to be thrown in a hurry – for instance, it may need to be thrown to someone in the water who needs help. In this case you cannot waste time coiling the line really well, but a few brief moments trying to make sure that the line is reasonably clear could be worthwhile.

THROWING A LINE

1. Coil the line carefully, taking care to get all the kinks out of it.

2. Transfer the coils to the left hand, making sure that they will run out freely. Keep about four coils in your right hand.

3. Turn sideways to the direction of throw, and throw underarm, or whichever way you find easiest.

1 2 3

COILING A LINE, CATCHING A TURN AND THROWING A LINE ARE ALL SIMPLE BUT ESSENTIAL ASPECTS OF SEAMANSHIP THAT REALLY SHOULD BE LEARNED BY EVERYONE AFLOAT.

Knots

There are very many kinds of knot, but for most purposes at sea, you will only need to know how to tie seven of them.

Most knots have a special purpose, and a proper knot should be easy to tie, easy to untie (which can be just as important, especially in an emergency) and of course it should not slip.

☐ You will get to recognise what sort of knot is needed for any particular job, and then you should be able to tie that knot quickly and easily without really having to think about it.

▲ REEF KNOT
Originally for tying reefs in sails, but also for joining ropes of the same size.

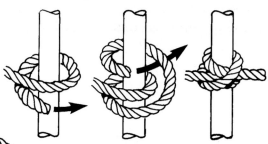

▲ CLOVE HITCH
For securing a line to a rail or ring.

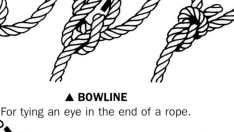

▲ BOWLINE
For tying an eye in the end of a rope.

▲ ROLLING HITCH
Secures a rope to a rail or another rope: can take a sideways pull without slipping

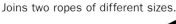

▲ SHEET BEND
Joins two ropes of different sizes.

▲ FIGURE OF EIGHT
Used as a stopper knot at the end of a line.

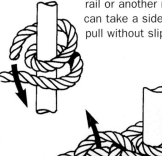

▲ ROUND TURN AND TWO HALF HITCHES
For securing a line to a ring or rail. Easy to let go.

CHAPTER 5

Getting Ready for Sea

Before a boat leaves harbour various routine things need to be done to make sure that she *is* 'ready for sea' and that there is a trouble-free day's sailing ahead of you. It is not just a matter of throwing off the lines and getting going.

There are certain tasks that the skipper will do himself, or he will ask another member of the crew to do, such as checking the engine and making sure there is enough fuel and fresh water on board, as well as the important matter of seeing that there is enough to eat and drink. A weather forecast is needed, and the skipper will have planned the day's passage, noted the times of the tide and possibly plotted a track on the chart.

These are some of the things that the crew have to do:

☐ Down below, all loose gear (including your own) needs to be stowed away, and all the lockers should be properly shut. Everything in the galley needs to be put away – sometimes the galley sink can be a convenient sea stowage for anything that does not seem to have a home of its own.

☐ Hatches and portholes must be closed and screwed down.

☐ On deck any loose gear such as the boathook and the dinghy's oars must be lashed, or stowed below so that there is no chance of anything falling overboard. You will soon find out what should be stowed where.

☐ Keep an eye open for loose gear at all times while you are sailing – both on deck and below.

The sails

The engine will almost always be used for leaving harbour but the sails will be prepared for hoisting before you leave.

☐ The mainsail cover has to be removed. The fastenings are undone, it is neatly folded up while it is still on the boom, then taken off and stowed. This is much easier than taking it off the boom and then trying to fold it, especially if it is windy.

☐ The main halyard will be shackled to the head of the sail, and then the slack on the halyard hauled in so there is no chance of it becoming entangled before it is hoisted.

☐ With a roller furling jib, the sheets will already be tied on, and they are led down through blocks on either side of the deck and then back to the cockpit ready for use. If the jib is not roller furling, the sheets are attached after the sail is secured to the forestay.

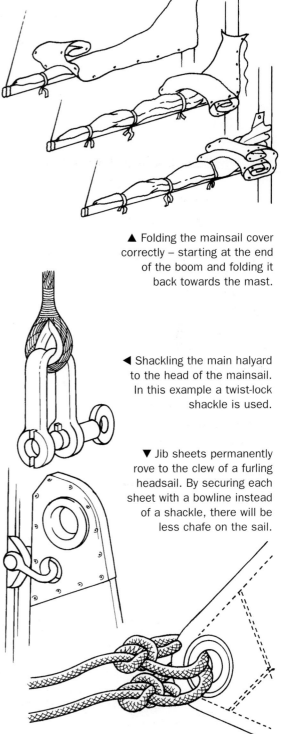

▲ Folding the mainsail cover correctly – starting at the end of the boom and folding it back towards the mast.

◄ Shackling the main halyard to the head of the mainsail. In this example a twist-lock shackle is used.

▼ Jib sheets permanently rove to the clew of a furling headsail. By securing each sheet with a bowline instead of a shackle, there will be less chafe on the sail.

Getting yourself ready

You need to get yourself suitably dressed, depending on the weather, **before you start**. Don't get cold because you have not put on enough warm clothing (keep the sea sickness at bay) and you certainly do not want to get drenched by the first dollop of spray before putting on your waterproof gear. No doubt you will take your lead from others in the crew as you may not want to be wearing full oilskins when the others are still in T-shirts. But it is far better to be overdressed and then peel off the outer layer when you find that the weather is better than expected.

Leaving from alongside

Do not take off any lines to the shore until the skipper asks you to. When the time comes to leave, you may be lucky and find someone helpful on the dockside who will let go your lines, but one of the crew can usually let go the last line ashore and still have time to push the boat off and jump aboard.

▲ As soon as you are clear of the dock, get all the fenders inboard. It is always said that a boat looks slovenly if she is under way with her fenders still hanging over the side.

Make up all the dock lines properly (see Chapter 4) and then stow them with the fenders (ask where). This will normally be in a cockpit locker or a locker in the stern, although fenders may also be lashed on deck. The sooner all the loose gear is off the deck, the better. Finally, have a last look around the deck to make sure that everything is secure and the boat is all ready to start sailing.

WHEN THE BOAT IS MOVING, AND YOU ARE HAULING IN MOORING LINES, MAKE SURE THAT THEY ARE NEVER TRAILING IN THE WATER, WITH THE RISK OF GETTING TANGLED IN THE PROPELLER.

LINES USED TO MOOR ALONGSIDE

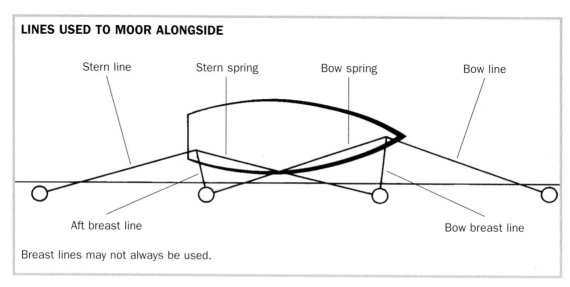

Stern line   Stern spring   Bow spring   Bow line

Aft breast line   Bow breast line

Breast lines may not always be used.

CASTING OFF MOORING LINES

When a boat is about to leave a dock, the skipper will say in which order he wants the mooring lines let go. It will depend on the situation, and especially on the strength and direction of the wind. Here is a typical instance.

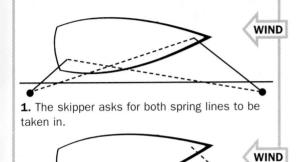

1. The skipper asks for both spring lines to be taken in.

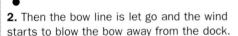

2. Then the bow line is let go and the wind starts to blow the bow away from the dock.

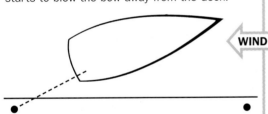

3. Finally, when he is ready to go ahead, the skipper asks for the stern line to be cast off.

Being safe at sea

When yachtsmen do get into trouble at sea they make the headlines, but many thousands of boats spend their summers afloat without any major incidents. Sailing is at least as safe as any other sport *provided you do not let accidents happen in the first place.*

For instance:

☐ By moving sensibly around the deck, wearing a harness whenever you are told to, or when it seems wise, and making quite sure that you never risk becoming a 'man overboard'. Remember: *'one hand for yourself and one for the ship'.*

☐ Being alert when things are moving on deck – like the mainsail boom moving from one side to the other. Keeping your fingers clear of ropes, winches and anchor chains.

☐ Using the stove carefully at all times, but especially in bad weather, and obeying the rules about cooking gas. The other aspect of safety is being able to cope with a problem if it should occur. As far as the new crew is concerned this means paying attention to any instructions from the skipper about safety equipment, getting to know where it is stowed and taking the trouble to learn how to use it.

Working around the boat

This is a good moment to mention this. You will generally find that your skipper, and the rest of the crew, like working on board with those who know what has to be done, and then get on with it. Which is why, with a good crew, life on board is cheerful and relaxed.

But, having said that, every skipper has his own ideas about the way things should be done and his regular crew will know this. To start with, and until you know the form, the right way for you to go about things is to ask first: for example, 'Shall I take off the mainsail cover?' In other words, showing that you understand what needs to be done, but at this stage asking for the skipper's OK before going ahead and doing it.

CHAPTER 6

Sailing the Boat

When you start to sail, you don't want to be hoisting sails
and pulling on sheets without knowing what you are trying
to achieve, so this chapter begins with a brief look at what a
boat is doing when it is sailing. If you have sailed a dinghy
you will know most of this already.

This is sailing...

You know that a sail is adjusted by its
sheet, so you can see that the way
the sails are adjusted (the way they are
set) depends on the direction the boat is
heading in relation to the wind.

☐ When sailing, a good sailor is
always aware of the direction of the
wind – relative to the direction he wants
to go – because it affects how fast he
can sail, and how easily.

This awareness of the wind is something
that you also will pick up quickly. You
will find that many boats have a wind
indicator at the masthead that makes it
easier to tell which direction the wind is
coming from.

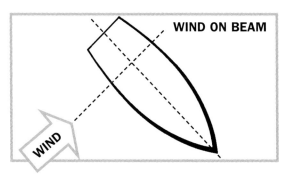

2. BOAT SAILING WITH WIND ON THE BEAM
When sailing with the wind on the beam, or coming
from the side, a boat is *reaching*. This is the
fastest and most comfortable point of sailing.

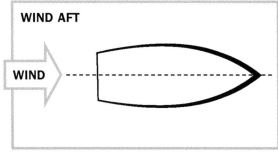

3. BOAT SAILING WITH WIND AFT
With the wind aft, the boat is said to be *running*.

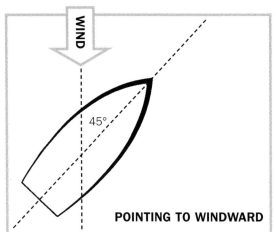

1. BOAT POINTING TO WINDWARD
Obviously a boat cannot sail directly into the wind.
The best it can do is sail at an angle of about 45
degrees to the wind's direction. When sailing to
windward like this a boat is said to be *on the wind*.

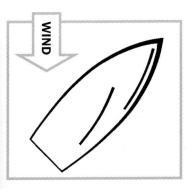

▲ When sailing into the wind, the sails are sheeted in hard.

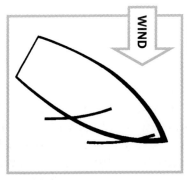

▲ When reaching, the sheets and the sails are eased.

▲ When running before wind, the sheets are eased even more.

A BOAT TACKING TO WINDWARD

Because she cannot sail directly into the wind, a boat making for a destination that is up wind has to steer a zigzag course. When she alters course to put the wind on the other bow she is said to be *tacking* or *going about*.

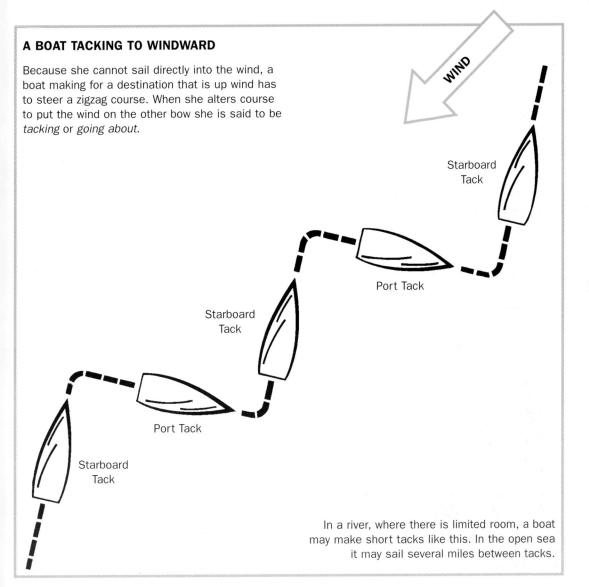

WIND

Starboard Tack

Port Tack

Starboard Tack

Port Tack

Starboard Tack

In a river, where there is limited room, a boat may make short tacks like this. In the open sea it may sail several miles between tacks.

Hoisting the mainsail

The skipper will normally use the engine to get clear of the marina or anchorage before hoisting sails. Then he will tell the crew when he is ready for them to start hoisting. Normally the mainsail will be hoisted first.

Unless your boat has a very small crew, you should find yourself – at least for the first couple of times – handling sails with someone who knows what to do. Watch what is being done, learn why it is being done, and be prepared to play your part as soon as you can. We will assume now that you have located:

- The *main halyard* and the *main halyard winch*
- The *topping lift*, and where it is secured on the mast
- The *vang* or *kicking strap*
- The *main sheet*.

If necessary, refer back to Chapter 3 to refresh your memory, or ask.

This is the drill for hoisting the mainsail. It may look complicated on paper, but it is easy when you put it into practice.

1. The halyard is shackled to the top of the sail to hoist it. Often this is done before leaving harbour.

2. The *sail ties* that are lashing the sail to the boom are taken off. These must be kept together and put in their regular stowage, ready for when the mainsail is lowered again.

3. The vang, if there is one, is eased off.

4. The skipper is told that the sail is ready to hoist. He will slow down, and point the boat directly into the wind, as it is almost impossible to hoist the sail unless the boat is head to wind.

5. When the word is given to hoist away, take hold of the main halyard, have a quick look up the mast to make sure that it is clear, and start hoisting.

6. The main sheet must be eased off as the sail is hoisted – it is difficult to hoist the sail if it is tight. If you are short-handed sometimes the helmsman can ease this for you.

Hanging a coiled halyard on a mast cleat.

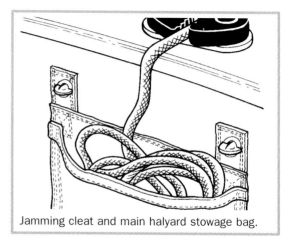

Jamming cleat and main halyard stowage bag.

HOISTING THE MAINSAIL

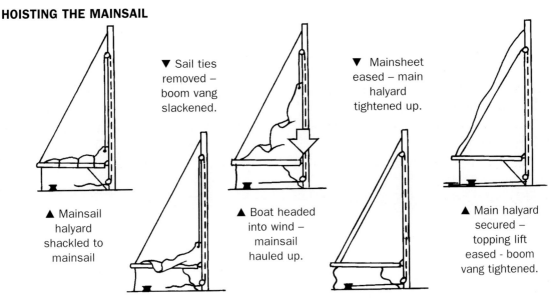

▼ Sail ties removed – boom vang slackened.

▼ Mainsheet eased – main halyard tightened up.

▲ Mainsail halyard shackled to mainsail

▲ Boat headed into wind – mainsail hauled up.

▲ Main halyard secured – topping lift eased - boom vang tightened.

7. As much as possible of the sail should be hoisted by hand – it may need a few good energetic heaves – because this is quicker. But as soon as the strain on the halyard becomes too much, catch three or four turns round the drum of the winch and insert the winch handle. Then, holding the halyard in one hand, wind with the other until the sail is right up and the *luff* is really tight. If necessary the skipper will say how tight he wants it.

8. Leaving the turns on the winch, secure the halyard on the appropriate cleat, remove the winch handle and stow it.

9. Ease off the topping lift until there is no weight on it, although it should not be too slack. Then make fast the boom vang.

It is important to tell the skipper (or the helmsman) as soon as the sail is hoisted and the halyard made fast. Because the boat will be pointing directly into the wind to let you hoist the sail easily, the sail will be shaking and slatting as it is hoisted. This is not good for the sail and the helmsman will want to *bear away* and let the wind fill the sail as soon as possible.

After the sail is hoisted, coil up the length of halyard now lying on the deck and secure the coil to the cleat. As well as keeping things tidy, this allows the halyard to run out clear when the sail is lowered again.

Some cruising boats have the kind of deck layout where the main halyard and other lines from the mast are led back to the cockpit. After it has been hoisted the halyard will then be jammed in its jamming cleat, and the halyard taken off the winch.

When jamming cleats for halyards are fitted at the cockpit, stowage bags are frequently used to stow the rest of the halyard. Once again, it needs to be out of the way, and ready to run freely when the sail is lowered.

Unfurling (*setting*) the headsail

Nowadays many cruising yachts have a roller furling headsail. In racing boats and those cruising boats without roller furling gear, the headsail is brought out of its bag, secured to the forestay and then hoisted. Eventually this is something you will have to learn, but to keep things simple, we will assume that your first boat is fitted with a roller furling headsail.

You will have seen that the headsail, when it is not set, is wound (furled) round the forestay like a blind. In effect, it is already hoisted and requires only to be unfurled. At the bottom of the stay is a drum for the furling line which is led aft down one side of the boat (usually the port side) to a winch in the cockpit. The sheets are left tied to the sail, and these also lead aft to the cockpit through blocks on either side of the deck.

1. When the skipper gives the word, the jib is unfurled by releasing the furling line and hauling in on the sheet. As the sail unwinds, so the furling line winds itself onto the drum, and it is best to keep just a slight tension on this line so that it is wound on to the drum tidily.
2. As the sail unfurls, the sheet is winched in as far as is needed.

Handling sheets on winches

1. If you are hauling in the sheet when the headsail is being unfurled, haul in as much as you can by hand. Then, *before a heavy strain comes on*, take three or four turns *clockwise* round the winch barrel. Make sure the turns are in the right direction.
2. With the turns safely on, insert the winch handle into its slot on the winch, haul in on the sheet with one hand, and wind in with the other until the sheet is correctly adjusted. With the turns left on the winch, the sheet is then secured to the appropriate cleat. While this is perfectly possible as a one-man operation, it is easier with two, especially if there is much strain

▲ With a roller-furling headsail, the jib sheets (**1**) are hauled to set the sail as the furling line (**2**) is taken up on the drum. To furl the sail the furling line (**3**) is hauled as the jib sheets (**4**) are slacked off.

USING THE SHEET WINCHES ON A BOAT SAFELY AND WITH CONFIDENCE IS ANOTHER BASIC CREW SKILL. BE SURE THAT YOU LEARN IT!

on the sheet. One person can pull on the sheet (*tail* it) while the other concentrates on winding in.

Self-tailing winches make single handed operation much easier. The tail of the sheet is jammed in the furrow at the top of the winch leaving you free to concentrate on winding in. Although the sheet may be jammed into the winch, the tail of the sheet should still be secured to a cleat when you have finished winding it in.

If there is a lot of weight on the sheet, the helmsman may help you by pointing the boat up into the wind for a few moments. This takes the weight off the sheet and lets you haul it in more easily. If you do get a *riding turn*, stop heaving in, or you will make things worse. You need to be careful clearing a riding turn when there is a lot of strain on the sheet. If possible get someone to help you, or ask for the boat to be headed into the wind for a few seconds. With the weight off the sheet you can take off the riding turn and start again.

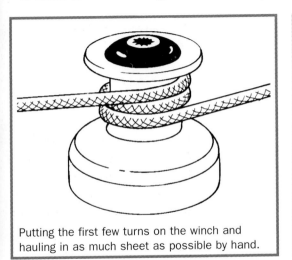

Putting the first few turns on the winch and hauling in as much sheet as possible by hand.

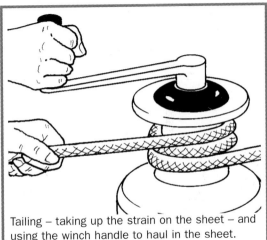

Tailing – taking up the strain on the sheet – and using the winch handle to haul in the sheet.

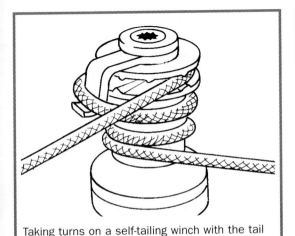

Taking turns on a self-tailing winch with the tail jammed into the groove at the top leaving the winchman free to concentrate on winding in.

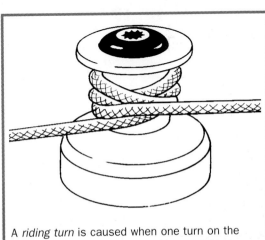

A *riding turn* is caused when one turn on the winch rides over another, and you need to be alert to see that this does not happen.

EVEN IN LIGHT WEATHER, THE WEIGHT ON THE SHEETS IN ANY BOAT CAN BE MUCH GREATER THAN YOU EXPECT — MUCH GREATER THAN IN A DINGHY, AND IN A FRESH BREEZE IT CAN BE CONSIDERABLE. THERE IS NO PROBLEM IF YOU CONCENTRATE AND FOLLOW THE RIGHT DRILL, BUT EVEN IN QUITE A SMALL BOAT, USING WINCHES CARELESSLY CAN MEAN MANGLED FINGERS.

Easing sheets (*letting them out*)

This must be done with caution, especially if there is much weight on the sheet.

1. Carefully take the turns off the cleat, keeping hold of the sheet and *keeping it firmly under control*. At this stage *do not take any turns off the winch.*
2. Holding the sheet in one hand, use the palm of the other hand other to ease the turns round the drum until the sheet is sufficiently eased. Keeping the hand flat saves fingers being caught.

If the wind is light, you may need to take one or two turns off the winch drum in order to ease the sheet, but this must be done with care, making sure you always have the sheet under control

Adjusting sheets

Earlier in the chapter you saw that the way the sails are set and the sheets adjusted depends on the boat's course in relation to the wind. We talk about *trimming* the sails. Sheets are *hard in* when sailing to windward, *eased* when you are reaching or running.

At first you will not be expected to know how sheets should be trimmed, although you will soon pick up a rough idea. The skipper or helmsman will say something like '*haul in the main*' or '*ease the jib*'. A modern boat reacts to quite fine adjustments to the sheets, and just a few centimetres in or out may cause a significant change in speed. Often there will be a speedometer dial in the cockpit which shows the effect on the

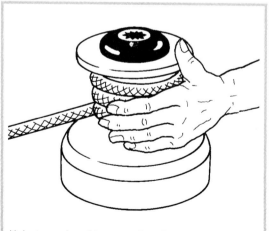

Using your hand to ease the sheet around the sheet winch.

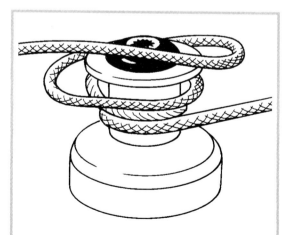

Taking turns off a winch by flicking the jib sheet over the winch.

ADJUSTING THE SHEETS

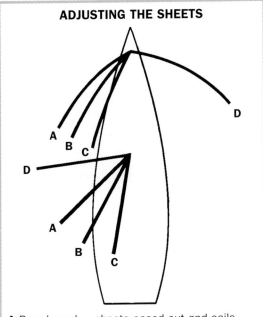

A Broad reach – sheets eased out and sails very full.
B Close reach – sheets taken in slightly, sails less full.
C Close hauled – sheets hardened in and sails flattened
D Running – sheets full out with wind from aft.

across is a cruising spinnaker (which is also known by various trade names).

These sails are made of lightweight material. They do not use a boom or a pole and are very easy to handle. The *tack* of the sail is secured to the deck right forward and the sail is hoisted on a spare halyard without being attached to the forestay. A single light sheet is led aft to the cockpit.

▲ Cruising spinnakers are only flown in light or moderate winds and when running or on a reach.

boat's speed when sheets are trimmed.

While you are cruising, there is unlikely to be the complete attention to speed and sheet trimming that is essential when racing, but if sails are not properly trimmed and kept drawing well the boat will go more slowly and you may end up in the wrong place. Most cruising sailors do like to sail their boats well.

Running

As you now know, running is sailing with the wind coming from aft. It is not always the easiest point of sailing, because if the wind is directly behind the boat – aft – it is difficult to keep a normal headsail full.

A sail that you are more likely to come

▲ A boat running before the wind with a spinnaker that uses a boom or spinnaker 'pole'.

CHAPTER 7

Sail Handling at Sea

The last chapter was an introduction to the most important part of this book – going to sea and starting to sail. Now, before settling down to enjoy your sail, there are three more basic and simple sail handling jobs that you should know. These are *tacking, gybing* and *reefing*.

Tacking ('*going about*')

The illustration in the last chapter (see p.38) showed that a boat can only sail towards the wind by steering a series of zigzag courses. And when she alters course in order to put the wind from one bow to another she is *tacking* – this is also known as *going about*.

The essential part of tacking is letting go the headsail sheet on one side and hauling it in on the other after the boat has changed course. Nothing needs to be done to the mainsail. Tacking can perfectly well be a one-man job, but is easier with two.

The jib sheets on either side of the boat are often referred to as the 'windward sheet' and the 'leeward sheet', but these change round after you tack and there could be confusion. So we will refer to the 'working sheet' – the sheet which at any time has the weight on it.

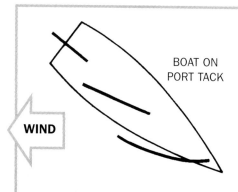

BOAT ON
PORT TACK

WIND

1. Ready about! – this is the helmsman's warning that he is about to go about.

TACKING THROUGH THE WIND

2. Lee oh! – as he starts to tack, the helmsman holds the tiller over in order to point the boat towards the wind. The crew is ready to let go the working headsail sheet. Nothing needs to be done to the mainsheet.

☐ The warning from the skipper or helmsman that he is going to tack is *'Stand by to go about'* or just *'Ready about'*. When he is actually putting the helm over to make the boat go about he'll say *'Lee-oh'*.

This is what you should do at each stage:

1. 'Ready about'

☐ See that the new working sheet is clear to haul in and take it round the winch in preparation.

☐ Take the present working sheet off the cleat, and stand by to let it go *but keep the turns on the winch until you are ready to tack.*

2. 'Lee-oh!'

☐ Wait a couple of seconds (no more) until the boat heads into the wind, then quickly take the turns off the working sheet (keeping your fingers clear!)

3. Through the wind – immediately the boat heads into the wind, the crew lets go the working sheet and moves across to haul in the the new working sheet. As the boat's bow passes through the wind the headsail will flutter until it fills on the opposite side.

☐ As the boat's bows pass through the wind, haul in the new working sheet. Take as much sheet in as possible by hand, *but be sure to take a couple of turns round the winch before the strain comes on it.* Then insert the winch handle and wind in as required to trim the sail. If you are going to windward this will mean 'hard in'.

If you are sailing short handed, let go the working sheet as you bring the boat head to wind, then move across to haul in the new working sheet on the other side. With two people crewing the boat, the one who lets go the working sheet can then move across to operate the winch handle on the other side.

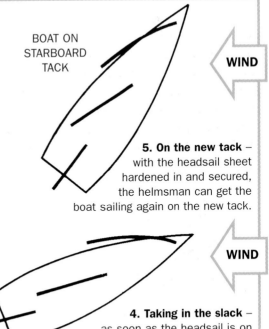

BOAT ON STARBOARD TACK

WIND

5. On the new tack – with the headsail sheet hardened in and secured, the helmsman can get the boat sailing again on the new tack.

WIND

4. Taking in the slack – as soon as the headsail is on the other side the crew hauls in the new working sheet as quickly as possible, first by hand, then with the winch. The helmsman may pause for a brief moment before completing the tack to make it easier to haul in the sheet.

Gybing

A boat gybes when she alters course so that the wind moves from one aft quarter to the other, i e the stern and not the bows will be moving through the wind this time. When gybing the mainsail moves across through the wind.

When the boat is running before the wind the main boom is eased right out, almost at right angles. When the course is altered so that the wind passes through the stern and comes from the opposite quarter, the boom will try to fly violently across the boat to the same position on the opposite beam. This can be dangerous and cause damage and injury, so an essential part of gybing is *keeping the boom junder control.*

But steering with the wind right aft can be tricky. It is only too easy to let the wind catch the wrong side of the mainsail and flip it over. To prevent this accidental gybe while running with the wind aft, some form of preventer is often rigged so that the boom cannot fly over accidentally.

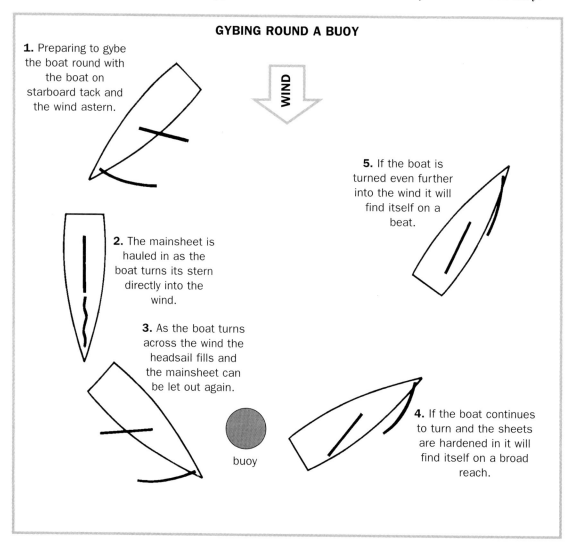

GYBING ROUND A BUOY

1. Preparing to gybe the boat round with the boat on starboard tack and the wind astern.

WIND

5. If the boat is turned even further into the wind it will find itself on a beat.

2. The mainsheet is hauled in as the boat turns its stern directly into the wind.

3. As the boat turns across the wind the headsail fills and the mainsheet can be let out again.

buoy

4. If the boat continues to turn and the sheets are hardened in it will find itself on a broad reach.

This may either be a line taken from the end of the boom up to the bow, or a tackle secured to the underside of the boom, with the lower block secured to the deck. Here is the drill for gybing:

1. 'Stand by to gybe' This is the warning from the skipper or the helmsman.

☐ The preventer, if one is rigged, must now be taken off.

☐ The boom is brought in by hauling on the main sheet until it is in the middle of the boat – amidships.

2. 'Gybe-oh!' This means the helmsman is about to alter course.

☐ As soon as the stern passes through the wind, the mainsail can be let out again on the other side, and the preventer is then rigged on the new side. By doing it in this way, the main boom is kept under control throughout the gybe.

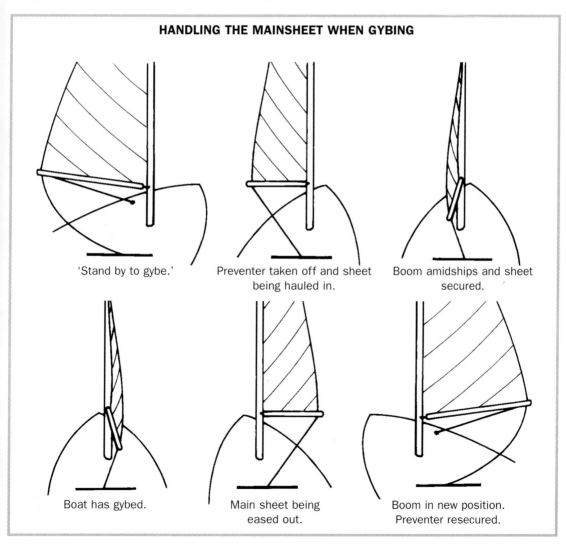

HANDLING THE MAINSHEET WHEN GYBING

'Stand by to gybe.'

Preventer taken off and sheet being hauled in.

Boom amidships and sheet secured.

Boat has gybed.

Main sheet being eased out.

Boom in new position. Preventer resecured.

Reefing

This means reducing the sail area when the wind is getting stronger. It may be natural to associate this situation with stormy weather, but often there is an advantage in reefing on a fine day when the breeze freshens.

It may seem good fun on a sunny day to be sailing along with the boat well heeled over and the lee side of the deck buried in the water. In these conditions you appear to be sailing fast, but by reducing the sail area slightly, the boat can be made to heel rather less and, in fact, will sail faster because you are not dragging the edge of the deck through the water.

Reefing the headsail

With a roller furling headsail, reefing is a simple procedure. The headsail sheet is eased while at the same time the furling line is wound in until the sail area is reduced to the size the skipper wants. Just how much the sail needs to be reefed depends on two factors – the wind conditions and judgement of the skipper – and it is for him to decide.

Reefing the mainsail

There are different ways of reefing a mainsail depending on the arrangement in each boat, but *slab reefing* is now the most common.

Look at the illustration of slab reefing and as in any other job on board, work out what you are trying to achieve. This is the drill:

1. Ease the main sheet so that weight is taken out of the sail.
2. Take up the weight of the boom by raising the topping lift – otherwise it will drop down when the main halyard is eased.

RELEASING THE JIB SHEET AND HAULING IN ON THE FURLING LINE TO REEF A ROLLER HEADSAIL

  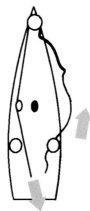 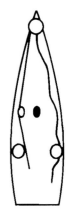

1. Take in the slack on the furling line before the sheet is released.

2. Release the sheet and begin to haul in the furling line.

3. Keep a light tension on the sheet to furl the sail neatly around the stay.

4. When the sail is furled, cleat the furling line and the sheet.

3. Ease off the main halyard and drop the sail until the point where you can put the *cringle* on the *luff* over the reefing hook on the mast or the gooseneck. (See the illustration)

4. Haul in on the reefing line until the leech cringle is pulled close down to the boom. (Look at the illustration again.)

5. Then hoist the main halyard until the luff of the sail is tight again.

6. Ease off the topping lift until there is no tension on it.

7. Adjust the main sheet as necessary to reset the sail.

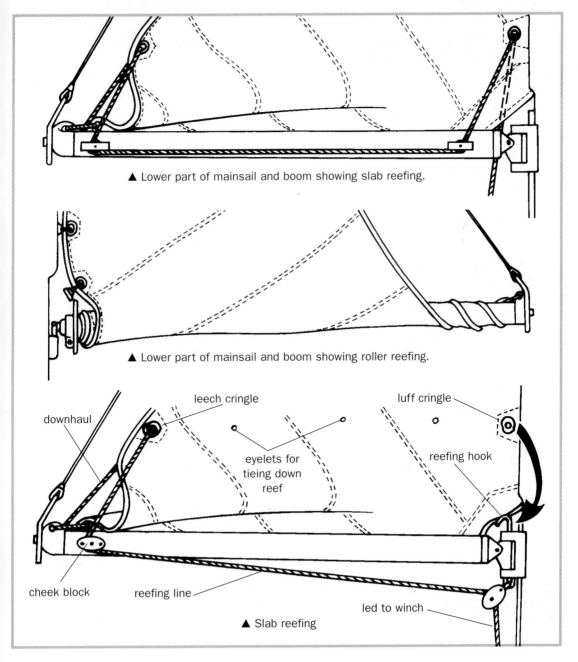

▲ Lower part of mainsail and boom showing slab reefing.

▲ Lower part of mainsail and boom showing roller reefing.

leech cringle

luff cringle

downhaul

eyelets for tieing down reef

reefing hook

cheek block

reefing line

led to winch

▲ Slab reefing

CHAPTER 8

At the Helm

Once the boat has settled down at sea, you will soon get the chance to steer. In fact, as soon as you are reasonably competent you will be expected to take your turn at steering (*take the helm*). Whether the boat has a wheel or a tiller, whoever is steering is said to be *at the helm* or *on the helm*.

If you have ever sailed in a dinghy you will find it very similar to steering a bigger boat, it is simply a matter of scale. And even if you have never steered any sort of boat before you will soon find it easy.

To begin with, the most common error is moving the wheel or the tiller too much.

STEERING WITH TILLER AND WHEEL

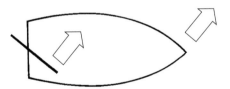

▲ To turn the boat to port the tiller is pushed over to starboard, as above. If you want to turn the boat to starboard the tiller is pushed over to port.

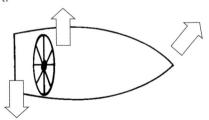

▲ To turn the boat to port the wheel is turned anti-clockwise to port, as above. If you want to turn the boat to starboard the wheel is turned clockwise to starboard.

Apart from altering course, the less you move the wheel or the tiller the better, because moving the rudder more than necessary slows down the boat.

Although you will soon be able to perform quite adequately at the helm, steering a good course when the boat is going to windward or steering in rough weather does require a little more practice.

To start with you will probably be given a visible mark to steer for – it might be a buoy or a point on the land. It is easier to steer for a mark that you can see, which will help you steer more accurately. But the time will come when you are out in the open sea, and there is nothing in sight to steer for. This is when you will have to steer by the compass.

There is a mark (sometimes a pin) on the compass mounting which is lined up with the bow. So when you alter course, the north point of the compass card stays where it is, and the lubber's line shows the new heading on the compass card. Compass courses are always given in numerals, not geographical directions: so if the course is south, you will be told to 'steer one eight zero, or 180 degrees. *Three* numerals are always used – thus 'zero one five'

The compass card is mounted on a pivot so that it always stays level and can rotate in any direction. There are magnets fixed under the card so that the North on the card always points towards the earth's magnetic north pole. In order to save space on the card, only two numerals are used, so that 170 is shown as 17.

▲ A typical compass card which is pivoted to swing easily within the compass housing. The North point will always point slightly to the left or right of *true north* towards *magnetic north*. This is called *compass variation*.

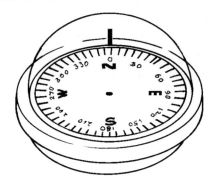

▲ A typical binnacle type steering compass showing the mark.

Steering to windward

When you are sailing, your destination will often lie to *windward* or *up wind*. We know that a boat cannot sail directly into the wind and sailing to within about 45 degrees of the direction of the wind is possibly the best that she can achieve.

☐ So, if you want to go to windward, you won't be able to steer a direct course. The skipper will want you to steer as close to the direction of the wind as you can – but still keeping the sails *full* (which means literally that they are 'full of wind' and not fluttering) and the boat still moving. This takes practice and concentration. You do it by watching the sails (and there may also be a wind indicator of some sort to help). You will be told that you are *pinching* if you are trying to sail too close to the wind, and not keeping the boat moving properly.

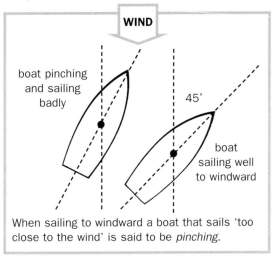

When sailing to windward a boat that sails 'too close to the wind' is said to be *pinching*.

While you are sailing to windward, therefore, you should mostly be watching the sails and not the compass, but you should also give an occasional glance at the compass to see what sort of average course you are able to steer. And when you have finished your spell at the helm, this course should be written in the log. The skipper (or whoever is doing the navigation) may be mostly relying on a GPS or other electronic gadget for his position, but as a back-up, he will want to keep a record of the courses *actually* steered so that they can be plotted.

On watch

When you are on the helm at sea, you are not only steering the boat, but you are also 'on watch', which means, if the skipper is not on deck, that the boat is in your charge for the time being until the skipper returns. If the crew is small and there is only one person on watch at a time, then there will be someone else 'on call' below.

On a longer passage or for a night at sea, the skipper will set up a formal system of watches so that everyone not only takes a turn 'on watch' but also can get some rest. For instance, you may have two hours on watch and then fours hours off. The watch system, including the length of the watches, will depend on the size of the crew. Arriving late on watch will definitely not be appreciated!

Being on watch entails more than just steering the boat in the right direction: there are other important matters for your attention.

☐ 'Keeping a good look-out' is not only good seamanship and good sense, but it is also required by law. The skipper will want to know at once if another vessel looks like coming close as he might have to take avoiding action, so all ships within sight need watching. These days, many large merchant ships travel fast and a vessel that seems to be a good distance away can suddenly become uncomfortably close. And don't forget to keep an eye out astern for anything coming up fast behind you! There is, in fact, a 'Rule of the Road', a kind of Highway Code of the sea, which states who has the right of way. But this is something to be learned in the future.

☐ Shore lights, buoys, land, or conspicuous landmarks on the shore, will all need to be reported to the skipper. You may be asked to watch out for a particular light or other mark which is due to come into view, although these sometimes appear unexpectedly.

☐ Finally, you will need to keep your '*weather eye*' open and we will talk more about this in the next chapter. For instance even a small change in the strength or direction of the wind may mean the sheets need to be adjusted and the skipper will certainly want to know if the weather looks like worsening.

Skippers rest or sleep more soundly if they are confident that whoever is on watch will immediately give them a shout if the situation changes in any way, or if there is the slightest uncertainty about what to do in any situation that may arise, and this procedure should always be followed.

But skippers need their sleep if they are to remain alert and effective. Sufficiently experienced helmsmen will get to know just when the skipper should be called or when the necessary action can be taken without disturbing him.

When your night watch gets towards its end, give your relief a shake ten minutes or so before he is due to relieve you, depending on how long he needs to get dressed. Do it quietly so that you don't wake the rest of the crew, and put the kettle on so that there is a hot drink ready for him if he wants it.

When you are on watch at night you have to be careful about using the boat's cabin lights because a bright light streaming up from the cabin into the cockpit will spoil your night vision and you will not be able to see anything on deck. So use a torch when you go below to look at the chart or call your relief, and don't turn on the cabin lights when you are called for your watch. The relief watch should be able to get dressed in the dark or by torchlight.

The autopilot

Many boats are fitted with an *autopilot*, an electronic device that takes the place of the helmsman and steers the boat. The desired course is set, the autopilot is engaged and off you go. This can be useful with a shorthanded crew, but autopilots use a lot of battery power, so the skipper may prefer, whenever possible, to use it only when the engine is running thus keeping the battery well charged.

If the autopilot is being used while you are on watch, there are two things you must remember while it is in operation.

☐ You must know *how to disengage it.* This will involve simply flicking an electrical switch in the cockpit. With the autopilot engaged you will not be able to move the helm, but you clearly must be able to do so if for any reason you need to alter course suddenly. For example, you may have to take action to avoid sailing into a fisherman's marker buoy.

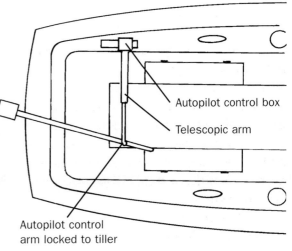

Autopilot control box

Telescopic arm

Autopilot control arm locked to tiller

▲ A typical electrically-driven autopilot.

☐ Although the autopilot may seem to be steering a good course (and it often does better than a human helmsman), you must *look at the compass* from time to time to make sure that it is still steering the boat in the right direction. Autopilots are usually very reliable, but like human beings, they have been known to go astray on accasions.

Playing safe

If you are alone on watch in the cockpit, either by day or at night, you must **never** leave the cockpit (for instance to go up to the foredeck), because if by any chance you slipped overboard, no one would know! If something needs to be done, call down for help.

In fact most skippers will insist that the helmsman always wears a safety harness at night or in bad weather. This starts with 'clipping on' while you are still down below and before you climb into the cockpit.

CHAPTER 9

Back to Harbour

You left harbour under power and you are likely to
return under power, so before entering harbour the skipper
will say when he wants the sails furled. You will also need
to prepare for going alongside a dock or anchoring,
depending on the plans during the day.

Furling the sails

Furling the headsail is easy. The sheet
is eased and the furling line taken to
a winch and hauled in. Rather than
letting go the sheet completely, it is
better to keep a slight pressure on it so
that the sail is not furled too loosely.

Furling the mainsail:

1. The crew members who are going
to furl the mainsail should each
provide themselves with a couple of
sail ties. Then the main halyard is
got ready for letting go.

> WHEN YOU ARE WORKING ON THE
> COACHROOF FURLING THE MAINSAIL,
> WATCH OUT FOR THE OPEN COMPANION-
> WAY. IT CAN BE HIDDEN BY THE SAIL
> WHEN IT DROPS AND YOU COULD EASILY
> FALL THROUGH IT. IT IS SENSIBLE TO
> CLOSE THE COMPANION WAY BEFORE
> WORKING ON THE COACHROOF.

2. The crew will tell the skipper as
soon as they are ready. He will alter
course so that the boat is heading
directly into the wind. At the same

time the main sheet will be hauled in
tight and the main halyard will be let
go. The sail should drop completely,
but occasionally it needs a tug to
help it down.

3. After the sail has dropped, the way
in which it is made up and lashed to
the boom will vary between boats
and will depend on the type of sail. It
may be folded like a concertina, or
with a lighter cloth the upper part of
the sail may just be gathered up and
tucked into the lower part before the
whole sail is lashed to the boom.

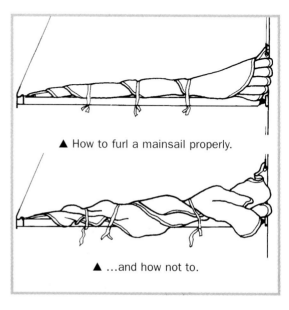

▲ How to furl a mainsail properly.

▲ ...and how not to.

Watch how it is done on your boat, but note that it *must be done neatly* with all the loose ends carefully tucked in. A neatly furled mainsail has somehow become one sign of a smart boat. Look around at other boats and you will see that the shabbiest boats always have badly furled mainsails.

If arrival in harbour is imminent and there is not enough time to furl the mainsail properly, it may be temporarily secured with three or four sail ties, and then furled properly after you have settled down in harbour.

Berthing alongside

When you return to harbour your boat will either berth alongside in a marina or at a dock, or she will anchor or pick up a mooring. In most cases the skipper will know in advance which it is going to be, but sometimes you may have to wait until you arrive to see what is available.

We will start off by seeing what is involved for the crew when going alongside, and deal with anchoring and

picking up a mooring in the next chapter

Berthing alongside a marina or a dock, and leaving it again, is a matter of routine but it is an important job for the crew.

There is really nothing to it, but if you keep your eyes open sooner or later you will see a boat whose arrival alongside does not go entirely as planned! Even skippers who are expert boat handlers are dependent on their crew, especially on a windy day.

The diagram below shows the various lines used when berthing alongside.

In practice, the arrangement of lines will not always be quite as tidy as it is in the diagram. In a marina there are likely to be enough cleats on the pontoons, but at some commercial docks you have to make do with whatever is at hand, e.g. rings or posts that may not be in the most convenient places.

☐ *'Mooring lines', 'berthing lines', 'dock lines', and 'warps'* – you may hear all these terms, but *'mooring line'* is the most usual term used and we will settle for that.

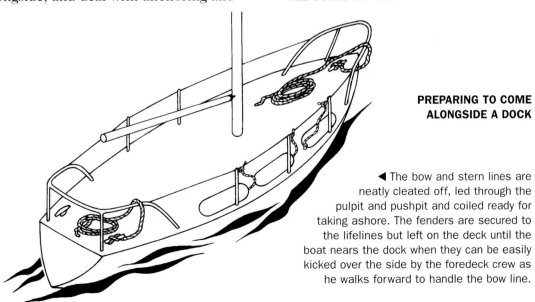

PREPARING TO COME ALONGSIDE A DOCK

◀ The bow and stern lines are neatly cleated off, led through the pulpit and pushpit and coiled ready for taking ashore. The fenders are secured to the lifelines but left on the deck until the boat nears the dock when they can be easily kicked over the side by the foredeck crew as he walks forward to handle the bow line.

Fenders

There are two different types of yacht fender, and their lanyards can be rigged in two different ways.

It is usual to attach three or four fenders over the side of the boat, and then adjust their position when you are finally berthed alongside. It is clear that the

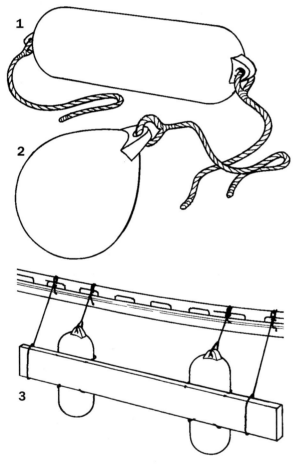

1. On this fender lanyards are secured at each end of the fender so that it can be slung either vertically or horizontally.

2. A fender with a single lanyard for hanging vertically.

3. Here two fenders have been used with a plank for mooring against vertical piles.

most important part of the hull which needs protection is where the boat's beam is widest, and the skipper may well advise you where the fenders are best placed. The height at which the fenders are slung depends on where you are going to berth.

Getting ready to go alongside

The circumstances of coming alongside may vary considerably. For instance, returning to the boat's home berth in a marina on a calm day should be quite simple. You know where the lines will go and, with any luck, there will be someone on the dock to help.

But going to a strange berth can be quite different, especially if it is not in a marina or if there is a fresh wind. You will not know where lines can be secured ashore, or if there will be anyone ashore to take them. And if there is anyone who wants to help, there is always a chance that they won't know what to do with your line once you have passed it to them! So the crew needs to understand the basic drill well – then prepare to be flexible.

This is the drill:

☐ Get lines and fenders ready on deck. The skipper may know which side of the boat will be alongside the dock – whether you will be '*starboard side to*' or '*port side to*' – so that you can get ready accordingly. But in a new harbour, it may not be clear until the last moment. In this case the skipper will hold off and wait until the crew have lines and fenders ready on the appropriate side – although he may still expect them do this as quickly as possible!

☐ Before coming alongside, the bow line and stern line should be rigged as shown in the drawing. The inboard end is secured to a cleat, and the line is led outboard, under the pulpit, then back in over the pulpit or lifelines, and coiled ready to be thrown or taken to the shore.

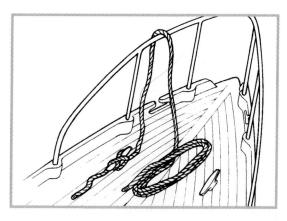

▲ A bow line rigged through the pulpit in preparation for coming alongside.

☐ Many boats' mooring lines have an eye spliced at one end, and that is the end to pass ashore. If there are no eyes, tie in an eye with a bowline (see p. 33) – say 18 in or 50 cm. If in doubt, or it is not obvious what is needed, ask the skipper.

☐ With more than one crew member (in addition to the helmsman) one can be ready with the bow line and one with the stern line. If you are short-handed and there is only one crew member, the skipper will say which line he wants secured first – and this will almost always be the bow line.

☐ In Chapter 4 you were shown how to throw a line. This can be especially important on a windy day when the boat may be blown away from the dock if you do not get your line ashore first time. (If you are not quite sure about your line throwing, it's a good idea to put in a bit of practice before it's needed.)

☐ If there is no one ashore to take your lines, a member of the crew will have to jump ashore with a line. Spectacular leaps are not encouraged as they may well end in embarrassment and injury. A more cautious, but more successful effort when the boat is close alongside is strongly recommended!

The usual routine is to get the boat secure alongside with a couple of lines – probably the head and stern lines. Then, after consulting the skipper, you can take your time to rig the other lines, adjust the fenders if necessary and finish with the boat safe and soundly moored. In bad weather or in an exposed berth, the skipper may want to rig additional lines – this is called *doubling up*.

AS THE BOAT APPROACHES THE DOCK AND YOU ARE AT THE BOW WAITING TO STEP ASHORE OR THROW A LINE, IT IS VERY EASY TO STAND EXACTLY IN THE WRONG PLACE BLOCKING THE SKIPPER'S VIEW. WATCH OUT FOR THIS AND AVOID HIS RUDE REMARKS. STANDING CLOSE TO THE MAST UNTIL THE LAST MOMENT IS A BETTER PLACE.

BERTHED ALONGSIDE ANOTHER BOAT

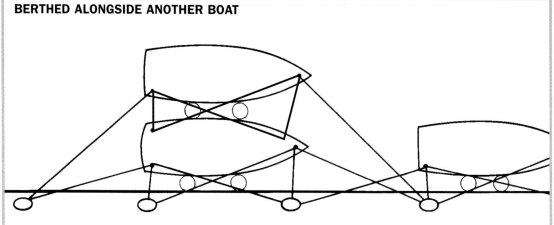

When you are berthed alongside another boat, it will be usual (unless she is much bigger than you) to put your own bow and stern lines out to the shore.

Also, when you are berthed alongside another vessel, it is considered bad manners to cross through the other boat's cockpit in order to get to the shore. The usual practice is to go ashore by crossing round the foredeck of the shoreside vessel – and always quietly.

Tidying up or 'squaring off'

When you have returned to harbour after a day's sail, whether you are alongside or at anchor, there is a natural inclination to relax. If it has been a hard day, you will want to get below and out of your foul weather gear; a cup of tea may be an attractive idea. But the boat must be squared off and left tidy and secure. It only takes a few minutes and all the crew must help.

☐ If you are alongside a dock or another boat, the inboard ends of all the mooring lines should be coiled up and left tidy. The next chapter will remind you about correctly securing the anchor gear.

☐ If there wasn't time to furl the mainsail properly before you came into harbour, now is the time to make a decent job of it. Some skippers like to put on the mainsail cover every time they return to harbour, others will not put replace it until the end of the cruise when the boat is left.

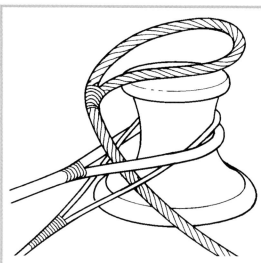

When there are already lines from other boats on the shoreside cleat or bollard, this is how yours is rigged. The eye of the new line is dipped through the eye that is there already, then slipped over the cleat. In this way any line can be removed without disturbing the other.

☐ The end of the mainsheet will need making up – ask the skipper how he likes it done. Any other sheets or loose gear will need tidying up or stowing. Any gear left in the cockpit should be stowed away below.

☐ Halyards! You do not have to be around boats for very long before you will hear the noise of a loose halyard slatting against a metal mast in the wind. This can be very aggravating in your own boat if you are trying to sleep and even more so for any nearby neighbours trying to do the same. To avoid this, halyards are always *frapped* (secured) away from the mast.

Making up a mainsheet
There are various ways to do this – this is only one of them.

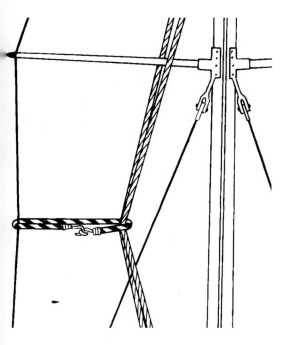

▲ The best way to keep halyards silent is to frap them to the shrouds like this. A spare sail tie or shockcord does very well.

☐ If you are at anchor, the dinghy is likely to be needed and must be launched (see Chapter 11).

Packing up

Suppose, for instance, you have spent a weekend sailing. It is Sunday evening and your boat has returned to its berth. The crew want to get home; there may be trains to catch, traffic to avoid, Monday morning to consider. But they cannot just walk ashore and leave the boat.

There are sail covers to be secured, garbage to be put ashore, perishable food to be disposed of, the galley and the heads to be left clean. Movable gear must be taken off the deck, the seacocks closed and the gas tap turned off before the boat is finally locked up. All this need not take long, and in a well organised boat this work will have started on the way back to harbour.

But it does have to be done, and the crew member who develops an urgent reason to depart ashore before the job is finished may not get asked again!

CHAPTER 10

Anchoring & Mooring

Successful anchor work means teamwork, with the skipper manoeuvring the boat and the crew handling the anchor gear on the foredeck. It works best if the crew on the foredeck always let the skipper know what is happening without having to be prompted.

The gear

Boats may use either rope (this is usually nylon because it stretches and provides more 'give') or chain for their anchors. Where rope is used there should always be a length of chain attached at its outer end between the anchor and the anchor rope. This is for two reasons: firstly the chain will prevent the rope chafing on the sea bottom, particularly in rocky areas, and secondly, the weight of the chain will help to achieve a horizontal pull on the anchor to make it hold properly. Whether a boat uses chain for its anchor, or a mixture of chain and rope, it is usual (just to confuse you!) to refer to it as 'the anchor cable'.

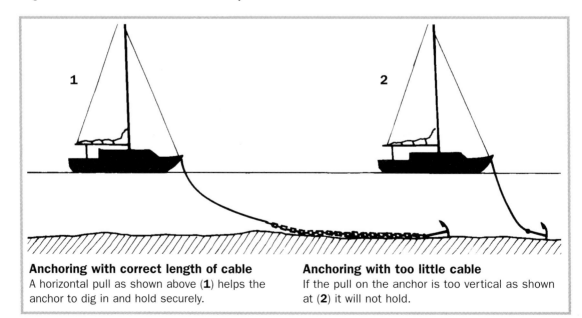

Anchoring with correct length of cable
A horizontal pull as shown above (**1**) helps the anchor to dig in and hold securely.

Anchoring with too little cable
If the pull on the anchor is too vertical as shown at (**2**) it will not hold.

Getting ready to anchor

The skipper will warn the crew to get the anchor gear ready, and he should say roughly how much line or chain will be needed. This is likely to be around five times the depth of water if the anchor cable is line, but rather less for a cable which is all chain, although this will depend on the local conditions and on the weather. Allowance also has to be made for the rise and fall of the tide.

In some boats where chain only is used for the anchor, the chain may be let go direct from the chain locker without bringing it up on deck first, but the usual drill is this:

☐ Bring up the required length of chain or line from the locker and lay it out along the deck so that it will run out easily when the anchor is let go. In most boats the chain and the anchor line is marked (for instance every five metres) so that you can tell at a glance how much you have on deck and how much is out when the anchor is down.

☐ Once you have enough chain or line ready, secure the inboard end to a cleat to stop more running out.

☐ Lead the chain through the *bow roller* (see illustration), make sure that it is shackled to the anchor, and that the shackle pin is tight. In some boats you may find a short length of wire used to secure the shackle pin so that it cannot come loose.

☐ Position the anchor where it can be let go as soon as the skipper gives the word. The best place for this will depend on the deck layout.

☐ Tell the skipper as soon as you are ready to let go the anchor.

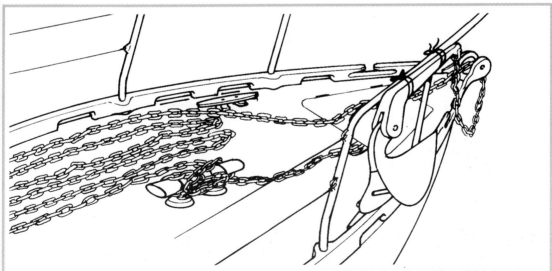

The foredeck showing the anchor chain flaked out on the deck. The inboard end is secured to a cleat while the outer end is led through the bow roller and shackled to the anchor which is temporarily lashed to the pulpit ready for quick release when the anchor needs to be dropped.

Letting go

It is possible to anchor under sail, but nowadays it is almost always done under engine. The skipper will manoeuvre the boat into the chosen spot, stop, give the engine a kick astern, and give the order to 'let go' just as the boat is starting to move slowly astern. It is essential that the line/chain is paid out bit by bit as the boat goes astern and not dropped in a heap, otherwise it will not hold properly.

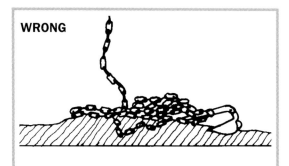

WRONG

▲ An anchor chain incorrectly dropped in a heap. This occurs when too much chain is let go too quickly, especially if the boat is hardly moving. It is unlikely that this anchor will dig into the seabed even when the boat begins to drift with the tide.

RIGHT

▲ An anchor chain properly paid out; the chain is let out steadily as the boat drops back from its anchoring point. This anchor will dig into the seabed successfully and hold securely.

TAKE CARE TO KEEP YOUR FEET, AND YOUR FINGERS, CLEAR OF THE LINE OR CHAIN AS IT PAYS OUT!

Is the anchor holding?

When the required amount of line/chain has been paid out, catch a turn (Chapter 4 shows you how to do this if you need a reminder), and look to see if the anchor is holding.

With a little experience you will be able to tell if it is: the boat will swing up into the wind and stop moving astern.

Sometimes the skipper will give the boat another quick kick astern with the engine to make sure that the anchor is well dug in.

Looking at two objects in line on the shore is a simple way of seeing if the boat is still moving astern and whether the anchor is holding.

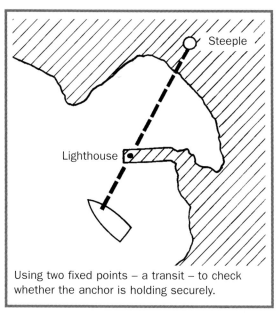

Steeple

Lighthouse

Using two fixed points – a transit – to check whether the anchor is holding securely.

Let the skipper know when you are finally anchored; he may come up to the fore-deck and have a look for himself. If he is satisfied that the anchor is holding and that there is enough line or chain out, bring up enough extra chain to turn it up well on the bow cleats, with at least one jamming turn, so that no more can run out. Chain is turned up on a cleat in the same way as rope.

If there is an anchor winch used for the anchor, it is not usual to let the winch take all the weight of the boat when it is at anchor. The chain should be taken off the winch and led to a nearby cleat on the foredeck, or some form of stopper may be used. Ask the skipper how he likes it arranged.

When anchored by night, yachts, like all vessels, should show a white anchor light forward – sometimes known as a *riding light*. Then they can be seen by anyone entering the anchorage after dark. Usually this means just switching on the white masthead light (but remember to switch it off in the morning). Some yachts have an electric anchor light that is plugged in and tied to the forestay.

By day, any vessel at anchor should correctly show a black *anchor ball* up forward. Usually only larger yachts will do this although merchant vessels always show an anchor ball.

The skipper's view

Finding a suitable place to anchor is the responsibility of the skipper, but you will always be a better crew if you understand what the skipper has to think about as he prepares to drop the anchor.

Several important factors should be considered when looking for the best spot to anchor.

☐ You need shelter from the wind and from a strong tidal stream. You also want calm water, if possible.

☐ The *holding ground* (sea bed) must be good so that the anchor digs in well. A muddy or sandy bottom is usually the best, and a rocky bottom is to be avoided. It is often difficult to get an anchor to dig into weed.

☐ The skipper can get the information he needs about the nature of the sea bottom from the chart. Cruising guides and pilot books also give useful advice about the nature of the holding ground in various anchorages.

☐ You want the right depth so that there is no need for too much anchor cable. But, in a tidal area, if you anchor near high water, you must, of course, still be afloat at low water.

☐ If you are going ashore, you will want to be near the landing, but it is better to have a secure anchorage and a longer dinghy trip.

Anchoring in a crowded anchorage – as many anchorages are today in summer – needs careful judgement. Where you let go the anchor is not where the boat will eventually lie after it drops back on the cable. An allowance must be made for enough *swinging room* in order to avoid other anchored craft, especially if the wind or tide changes.

☐ For this reason, when the skipper has decided where he wants to anchor and says 'let go', that is what he expects to happen. If the foredeck crew are not ready or are too slow, it is easy for the boat to drift out of position by the time the anchor *is* let go.

Weighing anchor – getting it back on board again

Do not start hauling in the anchor until the skipper is ready and tells you to begin. In order to speed things up and make it easy for the foredeck, the skipper will use the motor to put the boat directly over the anchor. In this way the slack on the line or chain can more easily be hauled in by hand.

☐ In order to achieve this, the crew must point down from the foredeck showing where the anchor cable is leading.

If you have enjoyed a secure anchorage, and a sound night's sleep, you may have to pay the penalty by finding your anchor really well dug in and difficult to *break out* of the mud or sand on the bottom. Boats fitted with an anchor winch have an advantage here because the added mechanical power will back up the manpower. But if you are relying solely on manpower and the anchor resists your attempts to break it out, the skipper may decide to use the engine to help break the anchor's hold.

In this case, haul in all the line/chain that you can, then catch a turn firmly on the bow cleat. Tell the skipper when this

PICKING UP THE ANCHOR

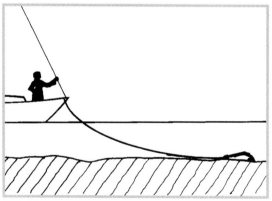

1. Boat's original position and its relationship to the position of the anchor – all slack hauled in.

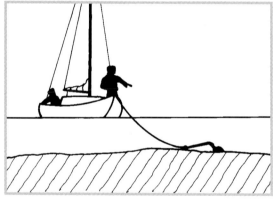

3. Figure in the bow pointing down to where the anchor is lying.

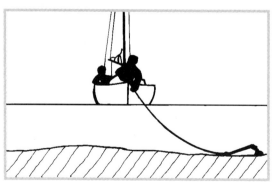

2. Boat beginning to motor up over the chain – crew taking in slack as it motors forward.

4. Boat positioned immediately over the dug-in anchor, allowing crew to easily haul in the slack.

has been done, and he will give the boat a nudge ahead with the engine which should free the anchor from the bottom. Tell the skipper as soon as it seems to be clear and complete hauling in.

☐ If you have been anchored where there is a muddy bottom you can end up with the chain and anchor coated with mud and weed. And you certainly do not want this mud on the deck or in the cable stowage. The cable is best cleaned with a stiff deck brush, and you may need to dip a bucket over the side and use sea water to help.

☐ If there is a lot of muck on the anchor, secure the chain/line then reach over the pulpit and try prodding it off with the boathook. If the anchor is not too heavy, you may then be able to lower it to the waterline and dunk it in the water a couple of times until it is clean. But take care that the anchor is not allowed to swing about and damage the boat's hull.

When anchor, chain and line are all on deck and clean, stow it away. If the anchor stows on deck or in the bow fairlead it will need lashing. Use a bucket of seawater to wash any remaining dirt off the deck.

At the start of this chapter we said that good liaison between the skipper and the foredeck was important. You will now see that this particularly applies to weighing anchor. 'Which way does the anchor cable lead?', 'Is the anchor coming clear?', 'Do you need time to clean it?' are the sort of things that the skipper will want to know. If he is given the information he will not have to ask.

A foul anchor

Just very occasionally you may be unlucky and bring up with the anchor more than you bargained for. In a crowded anchorage this could be another boat's anchor chain, or it could be some junk off the bottom. You will become aware that this is happening because the anchor will be hard to haul up. Happily this does not happen often; if it does, tell the skipper who will advise you how to sort it out.

▲ Clearing a foul anchor from an old mooring line by lifting it clear of the anchor with a boathook.

Getting moving

Correctly an anchor is said to be *aweigh* as soon as it is clear of the bottom. It is said to be *clear* (as opposed to *foul*) when it is out of the water and is clear of any entanglements.

You will realise that, as soon as the anchor is aweigh, a boat is free to move and can be carried by the wind and tide. On most occasions the anchorage will be sheltered, and although the skipper will have his engine running ready to move, the boat will sit quietly – even though the anchor is off the bottom. This gives time to clean the anchor and cable and stow away the gear before the boat moves, or moves at any speed.

But if there is a strong wind or tide in a crowded anchorage, there will be a risk of being swept into another boat and the skipper may decide to get moving slowly as soon as the anchor is aweigh. He should warn the crew about this.

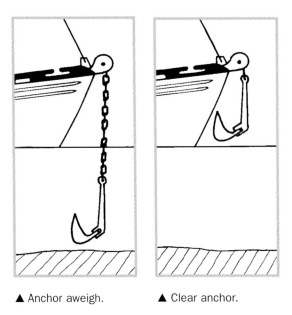

▲ Anchor aweigh.   ▲ Clear anchor.

Emergency anchoring

It does not happen very often, but there could be a time when you have to let go an anchor quickly in an emergency – for instance, if the engine packs up while you are in a crowded channel and you are unable to sail. Some boats carry a light kedge anchor on a line, and this can be thrown over quickly. If a kedge is not available, the main anchor must be let go. If there is a real hurry there will be no time to flake the line or chain on deck and you may have to trust to luck that it runs out smoothly!

Picking up a mooring

The purpose of mooring – to tether the boat to the ground – is the same as anchoring, so it fits well into this chapter.

There are various types of mooring, and if you are not sure what to expect when you pick one up, the skipper should be able to tell you. You may be picking up the boat's own mooring in her home port, or it could be a visitor's mooring during a cruise.

Occasionally the mooring will consist of a large buoy to which you attach your mooring line, but the illustration below shows a more typical arrangement with a smaller 'pick up' buoy attached to the main mooring buoy.

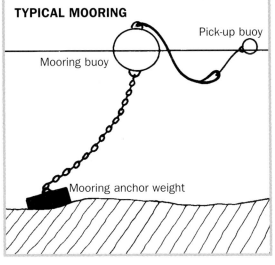

TYPICAL MOORING
Pick-up buoy
Mooring buoy
Mooring anchor weight

This smaller buoy is picked up from the foredeck with a boathook, and to make this easy the boat must be manoeuvred into the right position, This, once more, depends on good liaison between the skipper in the cockpit and the crew on the foredeck, because when the mooring buoy gets close up under the bows, the helmsman will no longer be able to see it. He will need to be told (clear signs from the foredeck will help) whether the buoy is to port or starboard of the bow, how far ahead it is, or whether he is coming up to it too fast.

Do not try to grapple the buoy itself, but pass the boathook under the small rope attached to it. Then bring the rope up to deck level and get your hands on the buoy. Bring the mooring line and the small buoy inboard **under the pulpit** so that the eye on the mooring line can go directly on to the deck cleat. A two man operation is useful here so that one can grab the boathook while the buoy is being hauled inboard: however it can be done by one person.

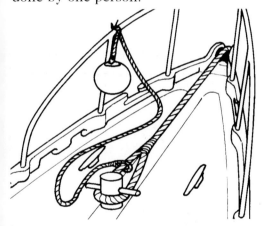

▲ Foredeck arrangement showing the pick-up mooring buoy brought aboard under the pulpit with the eye of the main mooring line led through the bow roller and secured to a cleat.

In a well rigged buoy, the mooring rope can be quite substantial, and it may have a length of plastic tube spliced into the eye to prevent chafe.

Once the mooring line is secured, it must be led through the bow fairlead. Some bow fairleads have a removable pin to prevent a line or chain from jumping out.

Slipping a mooring

This is a good deal quicker and easier than weighing anchor!

However you are secured to the buoy, do not let anything go until the skipper says it is all right to do so.

☐ If you are secured to the buoy with your own line, it should be rigged as a slip rope so that one end can be let go on board and the remainder pulled through the ring on the buoy.

☐ If there is a mooring rope from the buoy on board, the small pick-up buoy can be thrown overboard, making sure that there is nothing that will get caught when you cast off the main rope. When you get the word, cast off the main rope, taking good care that you do not get your fingers caught between the cleat and the eye of the rope, and tell the skipper as soon as it is clear. If the skipper cannot see it, point out where the buoy is when it is back in the water, because he will be taking care that it is nowhere near the propeller.

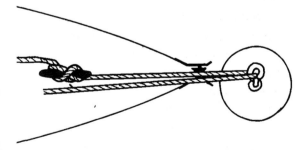

▲ Preparing to leave a mooring – one end of the bow line is secured to a cleat while the other is ready to slip through the mooring buoy ring.

CHAPTER 11

The Dinghy

The yacht's *tender* may be its formal name, but everyone will call it the 'dinghy'. If your yacht is lying at anchor or on a mooring, the dinghy is your only contact with the shore, and it is worth a short chapter on its own because the crew will find that they are much involved with it.

The dinghy at sea

We will assume your dinghy is an inflatable, but in the water a rigid dinghy is handled in exactly the same way.

For a short passage, and in good weather, the dinghy may be towed astern. It will usually be hauled in and towed alongside when you enter harbour.

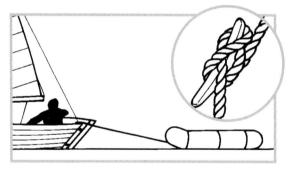

▲ Towing a dinghy with the painter securely jammed on a cleat.

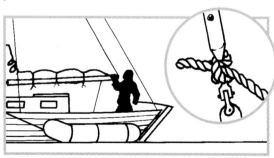

▲ The dinghy lashed alongside – the painter is secured to a shroud with a clove hitch.

☐ If you are responsible for securing a dinghy being towed, either astern or alongside, *make very sure that the tow is really secure!*

If there is enough room, a dinghy can be carried on deck semi-inflated, which saves pumping it up completely when it goes back in the water. But it needs to be very firmly lashed down as it can easily be blown away or washed over the side.

Inflation is easy with a foot pump, and the dinghy should be really firm, – but don't overdo it especially in summer because the air inside it will expand in the heat. When it is launched into the water *make sure that the end of the painter* (the line on the bow of the dinghy) *is still tied on board*, otherwise you might have to dive in and swim after it!

If an outboard motor is to be used, someone will be in the dinghy to receive it when it is passed down. This must be done with great care, even with a light motor – too many outboards get lost over the side each year. The motor should have a lanyard that is fastened on deck and not untied until the motor is safely in the dinghy. It should then be tied to the dinghy as soon as the motor is in place.

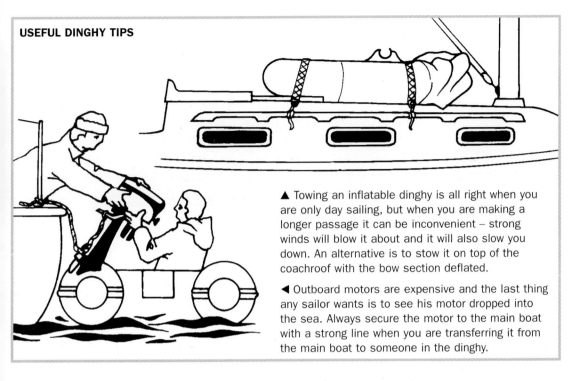

USEFUL DINGHY TIPS

▲ Towing an inflatable dinghy is all right when you are only day sailing, but when you are making a longer passage it can be inconvenient – strong winds will blow it about and it will also slow you down. An alternative is to stow it on top of the coachroof with the bow section deflated.

◀ Outboard motors are expensive and the last thing any sailor wants is to see his motor dropped into the sea. Always secure the motor to the main boat with a strong line when you are transferring it from the main boat to someone in the dinghy.

Handling the dinghy

Anyone who sails as crew must be able to handle a dinghy properly, *and this means being able to handle it with oars*, even though there is a motor. Outboard motors have been known to fail.

☐ Even if the dinghy has a motor, it must never leave the boat unless there is a pair of oars (or paddles) aboard as well.

☐ Whoever is handling the dinghy is responsible for seeing that there is enough fuel in the motor and that the oars (or paddles) are also on board.

☐ Many outboard motors have their own particular tricks to make them start. Does the motor need choke, and for how long? How much throttle will be needed before it starts? So, even if you have used an outboard before, find out about this one.

Taking the dinghy ashore

You will learn about the tide in Chapter 12, but meanwhile if you are handling a dinghy where there is a tide you have to be aware of what it is doing, especially if you are rowing. You need to be certain that you are able to row the dinghy against a strong tidal stream and how to make an allowance for the drift of the stream when you head for the shore, and again when you return to the boat.

☐ Before landing on a beach, when you are approaching shallow water, tilt the motor to avoid damaging the propeller on the seabed, and lock it in that position.

When you get ashore you must know whether the tide is rising or falling. If you land on a beach the dinghy should be carried up from the water's edge and parked above the high water mark. The oars should be stowed in the bottom of the dinghy

If you are securing the dinghy to a slipway or dock (other than a floating pontoon) you must make sure, with a falling tide, that you leave enough scope on the painter so that the boat will still remain afloat as the water drops. In the same way, with a rising tide, the point where you secure the dinghy should still, clearly, be above the water when you return.

When you come alongside the yacht, get the oars inboard as soon as possible to avoid scratching the topsides. Never leave the oars in their rowlocks; always stow them flat in the bottom of the dinghy.

Safety

Accidents happen far too often in dinghies, and quite frequently at night, when you should always carry a torch. Another major cause of trouble is overloading. A small dinghy will not carry a four man crew and all their gear so it is far better to make two safe trips from the shore to the boat than one risky one, even if it does take a little more time.

The skipper may insist that everybody wears a lifejacket in the dinghy, especially at night or in bad weather, and always for non-swimmers. These are sensible precautions – not sissy.

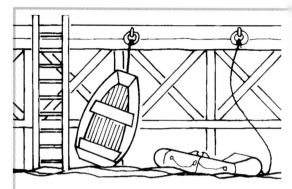

▲ At high water, allow plenty of rope when you tie up at a jetty, otherwise at low water you may find your dinghy in this situation.

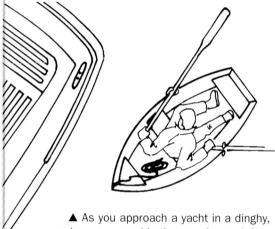

▲ As you approach a yacht in a dinghy, make sure you ship the oars in good time to avoid damaging the yacht's paintwork.

High water mark ▷

▲ The boat on the slipway is safe and secure, but the one left carelessly on the shore will float away as the tide rises.

RIGHT **WRONG**

▲ If you sit in the centre of a dinghy with an outboard motor, the weight will be more evenly distributed. It will not only be more comfortable, but will also perform more efficiently.

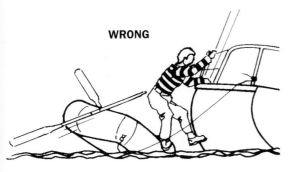

RIGHT **WRONG**

▲ Always try to distribute the weight in a dinghy evenly. Even in calm weather a badly loaded dinghy can be easily swamped by the wash from a passing boat. It is also harder to control.

WRONG

▼ As you approach the shore and get into shallow water, make sure you tilt up the outboard motor in good time to avoid damaging the propeller.

RIGHT

▲ Great care should be taken when climbing out of a dinghy on to a boat. This is not the way to do it.

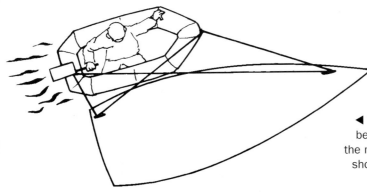

◀ The dinghy and outboard motor can be employed as an auxilliary engine if the main boat's engine fails. The dinghy should be securely lashed at the stern as illustrated in the diagram.

CHAPTER 12

The Weather & the Tide

Start sailing on the sea, and you soon find out what sailors have known for centuries – that when you are afloat you can never quite forget about the weather and the tide.

As the weather and the tide are both controlled by nature it is logical to talk about them in the same chapter. So let's look at the weather first.

The weather

Like any other sport, sailing is more enjoyable on a fine sunny day. But there is more to it than that. Not enough wind and you have to rely on the engine: too much wind and you can soon be wet and uncomfortable. And even with a 'nice sailing breeze', it depends on its direction. You will have a slow passage if it is 'on the nose', and a much faster one if the breeze is on the beam.

A great deal has been said about the weather at sea, but for the average cruising sailor it boils down to two things:

☐ Firstly, getting a forecast before sailing, and trying to know what to expect. How much wind will there be and from which direction? Is the sea likely to be calm or choppy? Is any change expected? All these things will indicate what the sailing conditions are likely to be. If plans are flexible, they can be changed to suit the weather and an advance forecast also allows you to decide not to sail at all if the conditions look unsuitable.

☐ Secondly, the skipper not only gets a weather forecast before going to sea, but he will also keep an eye on the weather while he is sailing. He will continue to listen to radio forecasts, but he will also watch what is going on around him, and try to be aware of any likely change.

All this is the skipper's responsibility, not the crew's: but the crew clearly has an interest in it all.

In most areas local marine forecasts are broadcast regularly by the Coastguard, and can be heard on the yacht's VHF radio. Forecasts are also posted up in yacht clubs and harbour or marina offices, and in every area there is a local Met office which will give you a forecast by 'phone. Finally, forecasts are regularly broadcast on local and national radio at set times.

Tonight

gales

15

1

6

clear skies -4

-3

5

15

▶ No doubt you sometimes see the weather maps that go with the TV weather forecasts. This map covers the whole country, so it cannot give full details of your area. But it does give a general picture of what to expect. For instance, this is a wintery scene with gales and rain off Western Scotland. In the south it is clear and cold with a 15 knot

Maps courtesy of **INTERNATIONAL WEATHER PRODUCTIONS The Met. Office**

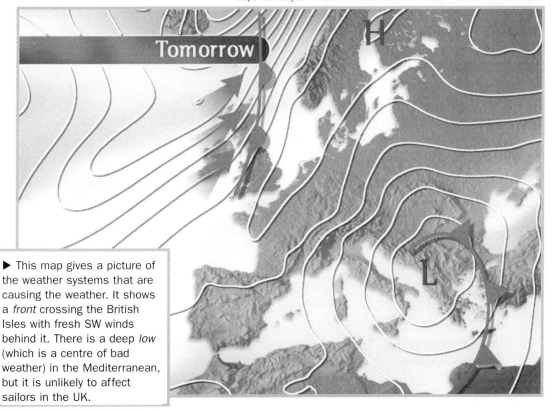

Tomorrow

H

L

▶ This map gives a picture of the weather systems that are causing the weather. It shows a *front* crossing the British Isles with fresh SW winds behind it. There is a deep *low* (which is a centre of bad weather) in the Mediterranean, but it is unlikely to affect sailors in the UK.

Do not be in too much of a hurry to blame the forecasters if they sometimes seem to get it wrong because the weather does not always obey the rules. Fronts and other moving weather patterns may unexpectedly change direction, or they may speed up or slow down. If you look out from your anchorage and see blue skies when the forecast is for wind and rain, that bad weather may still be on the way, just rather later than forecast.

Local geography can also affect the weather. For instance the wind tends to funnel up and down a river, and it is often diverted by high ground. So local weather can be different from the general pattern in the area.

Watching the weather

There are days when the weather looks completely settled. At other times it can change suddenly and it needs watching. A strong wind can blow out of a cloudless sky, but as a rule, approaching clouds or a change in the cloud pattern are the first visual sign of a change in the weather. Fluffy white cumulus clouds are mostly seen in fine weather, but it is the more sinister grey clouds that may mean worsening conditions. A change in wind direction can also be another warning of a change in the weather.

With modern forecasting and a careful skipper there is now less reason for a yacht to get *caught out* in bad weather. Most skippers like to plan their cruising so that, if there is a possibility of the weather changing for the worse, they will be within reach of a harbour where it is easy to take shelter. Nevertheless the unexpected can happen, and every boat

and every crew should be prepared to cope with bad weather if they should meet it.

The barometer

You will find a barometer aboard most yachts, and although it may be an old fashioned indicator of what the weather is going to do, it is still extremely useful.

Forget about the notations of 'Rain' or 'Fair' on some instruments: the important thing is how the barometer is moving. A steady barometer generally shows settled weather, and a rise in pressure is a sign of improving weather. If the barometer falls, the weather is likely to worsen. The faster it falls the sooner the bad weather may arrive, and the deeper the fall, the worse the weather may be. For this reason many skippers note the barometer reading in their log every couple of hours or so: then they can keep an eye on it to see how it is moving.

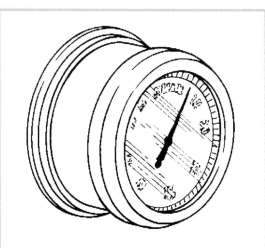

▲ A good skipper will always keep his eye on the barometer. If it begins to fall, he will have time to take the appropriate action, perhaps taking a reef in the mainsail, before the bad weather arrives.

THE BEAUFORT SCALE

| FORCE | AVERAGE SPEED | | DESCRIPTION |
	KNOTS	METRES PER SECOND	
1	1 – 3	0.3 – 1.5	Light air
2	4 – 6	1.6 - 3.3	Light breeze
3	7 – 10	3.4 – 5.4	Gentle breeze
4	11 – 16	5.5 – 7.9	Moderate breeze
5	17 – 21	8.0 – 10.7	Fresh breeze
6	22 – 27	10.8 – 13.8	Strong breeze
7	28 – 33	13.9 – 17.1	Near gale
8	34 – 40	17.2 – 20.7	Gale

The Beaufort scale

Even without going to sea you will hear 'Force 4' or 'Force 8' used in weather forecasts and in sailors' conversation. Admiral Sir Francis Beaufort was an early 19th century Royal Navy Hydrographer, who introduced the now internationally-used scale for wind and weather. While there is no need to learn it by heart, it is useful to have some idea of what at least the lower numbers signify.

A knot is the unit of speed used at sea and means 1 nautical mile per hour – slightly more than 1 mph. We will say more about knots in the next chapter.

The Beaufort Scale in fact goes as far as Force 12, which is a hurricane, but these higher numbers do not normally affect yachtsmen! The official descriptions can be misleading. We tend to think of a breeze as being quite gentle, but in fact Force 5, described as a 'fresh breeze', is more than enough wind for a small boat.

The tide

You do not need to know any technical details about the tide. These mostly affect the navigator and we will find out more about that in the next chapter. But almost as soon as you go afloat you can

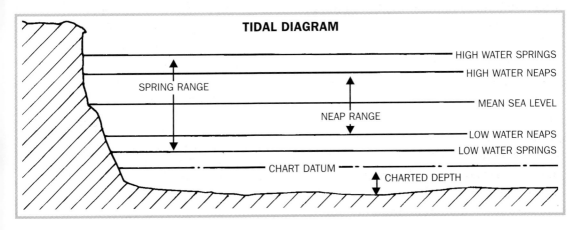

TIDAL DIAGRAM

HIGH WATER SPRINGS
HIGH WATER NEAPS
SPRING RANGE
MEAN SEA LEVEL
NEAP RANGE
LOW WATER NEAPS
LOW WATER SPRINGS
CHART DATUM
CHARTED DEPTH

hardly ignore the tide's effects if you are sailing in a tidal area.

Try rowing the dinghy ashore from a boat at anchor and you will soon know if you have the tide with you or against you. And once you get ashore you will have to decide how high to drag the dinghy up the beach or where to secure it at a dock – all of which depends on whether the tide is rising or falling. So let's sort out some basic facts.

☐ Sailors normally refer to high tide and low tide as *high water* and *low water*.

☐ In most areas there is a period of just over six hours between high water and low water – and then the next high water. However you can use local *tide tables* to find out the exact time of high and low water.

☐ The amount the tide rises and falls varies from day to day and from area to area. For instance on the same day in the UK it could be around 3 metres on the south coast and 8 metres in the Bristol Channel.

☐ As well as rising and falling, there is a horizontal movement of the tide called the tidal stream. When the level of the water in a harbour falls, the water must go somewhere

☐ When the tidal stream is moving towards high water, it is said to be *flooding*; and to be *ebbing* as it moves towards low water. So we also talk about the 'ebb' and the 'flood'. The tide is said to be *fair* or *foul* in relation to

the direction we want to sail, (ie the tide is with us or against us).

☐ At high water, the tide does not simply stop rising and then immediately start to fall. Nor does it instantly change direction at low water. At both high water and low water, there is a period called *slack water* when there is little movement. You can say that 'the tide is slack'.

☐ The movement of the tide is caused by the gravitational effect of the sun and moon on the earth. When the moon is new and when it is full (or two days later to be exact) we have *spring tides* when high water is higher than average and low water is lower than average. Soon after the first and third quarters of the moon we have *neap tides* when the rise and fall is least. It follows that tidal streams flow more strongly during spring tides and are weaker during neaps.

▲ You can see the effect of any tidal stream – in which direction the tide is flowing and how strong it is – as you sail past a buoy. Boats at anchor point into the tide (unless the wind is strong) and turn when the tide changes.

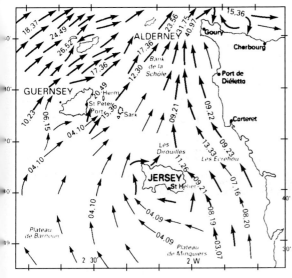

TIDAL STREAM CHARTS

Here are two tidal stream charts for the area around the Channel Islands, where the streams are particularly strong. There is a set of twelve charts, one for each hour before and after High Water at Dover.

The figures alongside some of the arrows indicate the strength of the stream in knots, with the higher figure at spring tides and the lower figure at neap tides.

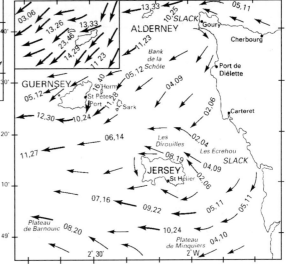

▲ This is the situation at four hours before High Water at Dover (which you would find from the tide tables). The stream is almost at its strongest at this time.

▶ This is the situation when it is exactly High Water at Dover. In most places the tide is flowing in a different direction.

The effects of the tide

The skipper will usually note the times of high and low water in the log each day. He may also note the *range* of the tide, ie the amount the tide is going to rise and fall, because there are many occasions when this will be important. For instance: if you anchor towards high water, will there still be enough water to stay afloat when the tide is low? Or will there be enough water for you to enter a particular harbour? And, as many interesting creeks and harbours are shallow, knowing the state of the tide is essential for you to be able to explore them. You have probably seen the tidal

stream flowing up and down a river near the sea.

The skipper can find information about the direction and speed of the tidal stream at any particular time from his books and charts (see the illustration above), and although there can be a tidal stream out in the open sea, its effect will be felt most in narrow channels and round some headlands. This is why the skipper might sometimes get you out of your bunk at what seems a ridiculous hour – because he wants to sail early to *catch a fair tide* out of the harbour or round a headland. When you set sail, in relation to the state of the tide, will make all the difference to your day's progress.

CHAPTER 13

Navigation

– or finding your way afloat

**Putting it very simply, navigation is the business of finding
your way from one place to another by boat. And you can
add: 'without actually hitting anything'!**

Usually you will find that the skipper does all the navigation, although sometimes he may delegate it to another member of the crew. As a newcomer you will clearly not be expected to know anything about navigating. But as soon as you have started to learn how to be a useful crew, you will probably want to find out what else is going on around you. So here is a a very simple introduction to what the navigator is trying to do.

Charts and books

When you look at a chart on a chart table you'll realise that it is a 'road map of the sea'. There are various types of chart, some published by the Admiralty Hydrographic Office and some by other commercial publishers. There are also large scale charts of harbours, charts which cover specific stretches of coast-line, and charts that cover whole oceans.

Take every opportunity to look at the chart that is being used because charts can be fascinating and there is a great deal to be learned from them.

If there is a moment to spare before you set sail ask to be shown the plan for the day on the chart. And at any time while you are sailing there will usually be a chance to ask the navigator where you are on the chart (or try to work it out for yourself), and then try to recognize any landmarks that may be in sight.

Start by noting these points:

☐ Different types of chart use different colour schemes, but the land areas are always a contrasting colour to the water, and shallow and deep water are also shown in different colours.

☐ The area covered by water is dotted with small figures. These are known as *soundings* and they show the least depth of the water (in metres) at that specific spot.

☐ There are many symbols used to indictate important features such as lighthouses, buoys, and obstructions, as well as conspicuous objects on the shore (eg churches or radio masts) which the navigator may find useful to identify to establish his position. Many of these chart symbols are self-

SECTION OF A TYPICAL CHART SHOWING THE ENTRANCE TO PORTSMOUTH HARBOUR

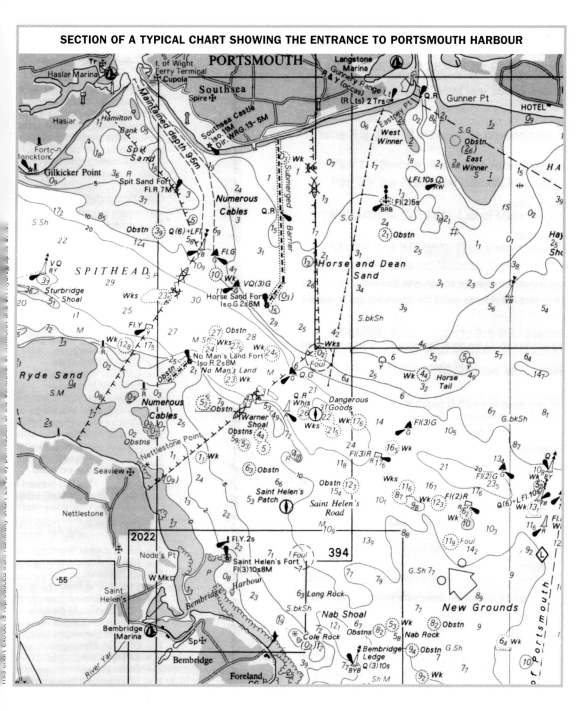

evident, but you can look up any that puzzle you. Chart symbols are also shown on the back of some commercial charts, in almanacs, and in other sailing reference books.

☐ Lighthouses and buoys with lights have a purple blip alongside them on the chart to differentiate them from unlit buoys. We will be talking more about lights later on.

While charts are probably the most important navigational reference, you may also want to browse through the bookshelf alongside the chart table, because there are two kinds of book which are also helpful. First of all every yacht carries some kind of *nautical almanac*. There are various types of almanac, but they all contain a great deal of useful information ranging from local tide tables and harbour information to more general reference material. If there is something that you want to look up you may well find it in the almanac.

The other type of book to look for is a *cruising guide*. These are marine guide books covering areas visited by yachts, and they combine navigation information (such as a description of the coastline and advice on entering the various harbours) with details of the facilities to be found ashore. You will find it well worthwhile browsing through a cruising guide that covers the area where you are sailing.

What is the depth?

When trying to find your way on land, you need to know where you are and then decide in which direction you want to go. But the sailor has an additional problem: he not only needs to know where he is, but he also needs to know the depth of the water under him. This does not usually matter when you are sailing far out at sea, but it can be very important when inshore, and when entering rivers and small harbours.

The amount of water that a yacht *draws* (its *draught*) is the depth of the bottom of the keel below the waterline. It might be between one and two metres, or slightly more. Obviously the navigator has to consider the boat's draught when sailing in shallow water.

CROSSING A BAR
BEFORE HIGH WATER

CROSSING A BAR AT
HIGH WATER

Buoys

You will sail past buoys and you will see them on the chart. They are there to guide ships by marking the channels in and out of harbours and to warn them of shallow water, rocks, or any other hazards. If you learn to recognize the various types, you will be able to look at a buoy on the water and understand why it is there and what it signifies.

The channel buoys you see as you sail into a large port will be marking the deep water channel for big ships, but there is likely to be enough water for a yacht to sail safely just outside the channel but close to it. However, there are also narrow channels in creeks and small harbours where a yacht would be wise to take care and keep inside the channel buoys. This is where the soundings marked on charts come in handy.

LATERAL MARKS

Direction of buoyage when entering harbour.

PORT HAND BUOYS
Various shapes
RED

STARBOARD HAND BUOYS
Various shapes
GREEN

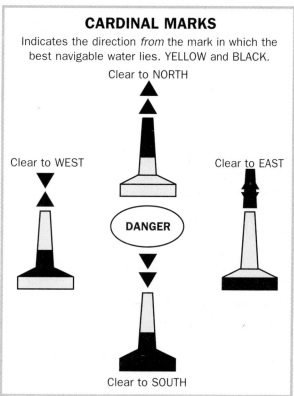

CARDINAL MARKS

Indicates the direction *from* the mark in which the best navigable water lies. YELLOW and BLACK.

Clear to NORTH

Clear to WEST

Clear to EAST

DANGER

Clear to SOUTH

ISOLATED DANGER MARK
Marking a specific danger with clear water all round. BLACK and RED.

SAFE WATER MARK
Usually positioned in the middle of a channel with clear water all round. RED vertical stripes on WHITE.

SPECIAL MARK
Not a navigation mark but indicating a special feature. Any shape with top mark 'X'. YELLOW.

OTHER IMPORTANT MARKS

Lights

When a sailor out at sea sees a lighthouse flashing, or when he sees a lighted buoy in a channel (where there may be many other lighted buoys), he needs to be able to identify that *particular* lighthouse or buoy. So each light has a different pattern of flashes, and this is marked alongside it on the chart. For instance, a buoy marked Fl 10s means that the light flashes once every 10 seconds. The chart also shows the light's colour, (red, green, white etc) and alongside a lighthouse you will see details giving the range of the light – the distance from which it is visible out at sea. This may be 10 miles or more.

PORTLAND BILL LIGHTHOUSE

Portland Bill lighthouse is a conspicuous landmark for sailors in the English Channel, and a clear warning at night.

The description on the chart says: **Fl (4) 20s 43m 25M** which means that the light shows four flashes every twenty seconds, it is 43 metres high and is visible for 25 miles.

In foggy weather, a fog horn sounds every thirty seconds.

The tides

In the last chapter we learned how much the tide can affect your sailing, but the navigator has to take a rather more precise view of what the tide is doing.

He can find out the times of local tides, high and low water, from the Tide Tables and he will probably note these in the log for quick reference. He will also want to know the tidal *range*, that is how much the tide is going to rise and fall. This is not constant in any area as it varies between springs and neaps. For example, if the boat drops anchor around high water, the navigator will want to know how far the tide will fall so that the boat will not be sitting on the bottom at low water.

It is also important to know how the tidal stream may affect the day's sailing. The navigator can find this out from a nautical almanac (and sometimes from the chart) where there are often inset tidal stream charts showing the direction and strength of the tidal stream for each hour in various areas (see p.79). These will be of particular interest if your route takes you where the tidal stream may be strong, such as round headlands and

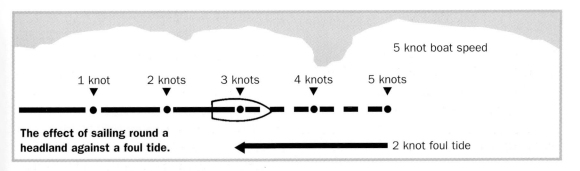

1 knot 2 knots 3 knots 4 knots 5 knots

5 knot boat speed

**The effect of sailing round a
headland against a foul tide.**

2 knot foul tide

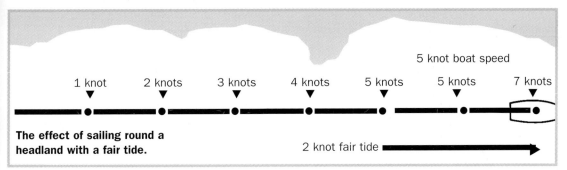

1 knot 2 knots 3 knots 4 knots 5 knots 5 knots 7 knots

5 knot boat speed

**The effect of sailing round a
headland with a fair tide.**

2 knot fair tide

through any narrow channels.

Suppose, for example, that you will be sailing past a headland and expect to be making a speed of about five knots. The information shows that, at the time you expect to be passing the headland, the tidal stream flowing round it will be about two knots (which is quite usual). If you round the headland with a *foul* tide you may be sailing at five knots, but with two knots of foul tide against you, the boat will be struggling past it at only three knots over the ground. However if the navigator has got it right and you sail with a *fair* tide, you can add two knots of tide to your sailing speed of five knots and you will rocket past the headland at seven knots. Even if you reach the headland when the tide is *slack* you can still make good your five knots. So there are times when planning to make the best use of the tide can get you into harbour in better time at the end of the day.

Measuring distance

Distance at sea is measured in *nautical miles (nm)*, and a nautical mile equals 2000 yards, so it is longer than the statute mile used ashore. Kilometres are not used at sea.

On some large scale charts there are distance scales similar to those on a road map. But a nautical mile is also equal to one minute of latitude, so, using a pair of dividers, distance can be measured from the latitude scale on the *side* of the chart.

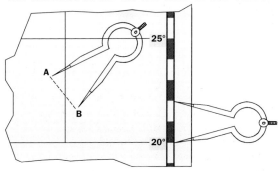

▲ Measuring distance on a chart with dividers.

Plotting courses

When a yacht is sailing close inshore with the land in sight and heading for something that is visible, for instance a buoy or a headland, the navigator can point out the visible feature to the helmsman and tell him to steer towards it.

But obviously there are going to be many occasions when this will not be possible and a compass course to the next planned destination will be needed.

So when he is sailing along a coast, or away from the land, the navigator will want to plot the course on the chart. This means that he will draw on the chart, using a soft pencil, the track that he wants to follow, either to the yacht's final destination or to the next point on the way.

On every chart you will see at least one *compass rose* like the one shown at the foot of the page. Using either a parallel ruler or some kind of chart plotter the navigator can use the compass rose to measure off the course he has just plotted, and then tell the helmsman to steer this course.

The compass rose can also be used if the navigator wants to take bearings of objects on the shore and plot those on the chart.

The gadgets

The most common electronic instrument used by the navigator is an *echo sounder*, which measures the depth of water under the boat. The instrument itself will usually be sited near the chart table, and there may also be a repeater in the cockpit. The *transducer,* which is out of sight in the bilges, is the part of the echo sounder that transmits sound impulses to the sea bottom which then bounce back to be picked up by the instrument and displayed on the echo sounder screen as the depth of water beneath the keel.

The most useful and important occasion to use an echo sounder is when entering harbour to check the depth of water, and for finding a suitable spot to anchor.

In many boats you will also see an electronic log and speedometer. There can be confusion in terms here. A log is an instrument (there are various types) for measuring the distance travelled by a boat through the water, but 'log' is also used as an abbreviation for the log book in which a vessel's navigational details are noted. You will

▲ You will see a compass rose like this on the chart.

find the log book on the chart table. The log reading, which tells you how far you have travelled through the water each hour, is useful for plotting a boat's position when sailing offshore or along the coast.

The speedometer is not much used for navigation, but the cockpit repeater is useful (and essential in racing boats) to show how the boat's speed changes when the sails are trimmed.

Electronic navigation

There is every chance that your boat will carry some sort of electronic navigation instrument such as a GPS (Global Positioning System) which gives the boat's position (in latitude and longitude) based on data it picks up from satellites. There may even be an electronic chart plotter with a screen showing the boat's position on the 'screen chart'.

All this is interesting and good fun and as it generally works well you may wonder if there is any need to learn the traditional methods of navigation. The answer is that electronic navigation equipment is a great help to the yachtsman, particularly when navigating out of sight of land or in poor visibility. But to make the best and safest use of it you do have to know basic navigation, and this can be important when you are navigating close inshore.

Furthermore, although electronic equipment is usually very reliable, it is not infallible, so you do need to check it regularly; should it fail you must be able to revert to the old methods of navigation. What would you do if the batteries fail and there is no power?

The navigator's day

Any day's sail needs some planning. Times of high and low water must be noted, the tidal stream checked, courses marked on the chart, and distances measured so that you have some idea when you will arrive at points along the route as well as your final destination.

The navigator will also look on the chart for any shallow water or other dangers to be avoided, and marks such as buoys and beacons that will help. If part of the plan is to visit a new harbour, he will read about it in one of the cruising guides.

It may seem obvious, but an important task for the navigator is to keep a constant check on where he is. This will occupy most of his time when sailing close to the land, especially in an area that he has not visited before and when entering a new harbour. He may sometimes use his GPS, or take compass bearings of objects on the shore, but much of it may be 'eyeball navigation' – making use of buoys and other marks.

When sailing away from the land he will probably plot the boat's position on the chart (a *fix*) every hour or half hour. He may get that position from his GPS. But the log book should also show a record of the courses that have been steered and the distance run as this information can be used to plot a position and compare it.

In a word – the navigator works out a safe, direct route to your destination. Then, because a good navigator never takes anything for granted, he uses all the information that he has available to check his position and make sure you are following that route.

CHAPTER 14

How to be a Good Crew

If you carry on sailing, and as you gain knowledge and experience, the chances are that you will want to become one of those sought-after characters – 'a good crew'.

An experienced skipper might think about it and say, when it comes to the crunch, that the really good crew is someone who copes well when the going gets tough, someone who is not seasick (or has his seasickness under control), can do a useful spell at the helm in a rough sea, can help tie the second reef in the mainsail, and can then go below and brew up hot soup for everyone.

But luckily most of our sailing is not in rough weather. When you are cruising there is no great welcome for the chap who may be strong and handy on deck but somehow cannot be classified as 'good to have aboard', which may mean that he doesn't do his share of the chores or fit in well with the rest of the crew. You will have discovered that living as a crew, so close to each other in a confined space, even if only for a few days, does require a bit of give and take.

Equally there is not often room in a small boat for passengers, who may be fun to have around, but who can create a disaster as soon as they get their hands

on a rope. So it might be said that the best person to sail with is a mixture of 'good seaman' and 'good shipmate', although he or she might not be thought of in such clear terms.

To be a good sailor you need knowledge and you also need experience. There are various formal courses organised by the RYA where you can acquire qualifications ranging from Competent Crew through to Offshore Skipper. The syllabus for these exams provide a guide to the knowledge you need to know.

A mark of the good sailor is that he can turn his hand to almost anything. He can splice an eye in a mooring line and is quite confident about going up the mast to deal with any problems up there. He also knows how to carry out a minor engine repair, check the state of the batteries, and deal with a leak in the heads. After all this he can cook an excellent supper – and leave the galley clean and tidy afterwards!

He may not be an expert navigator but he can certainly understand a chart and could get the boat safely back to harbour if anything happened to the skipper.

Finally, a good sailor always seems to have his eyes open and his wits about him. He may be relaxing in the cockpit with a mug of coffee or a can of beer and joining in the conversation. But somehow he will be the first to notice that a lashing on the dinghy is frayed or that the direction of the wind is changing.

This may make the good sailor sound like a Superman – almost too good to be true. But he or she is merely a practical sort of person who respects the sea, sees all the things that need to be done in a boat, and then learns to do them. This does not stop him from thoroughly enjoying himself, and being fun to sail with. Does he sound like you?

CHAPTER 15

Now do you Know...?

These are some of the things you will want to know if you go sailing. It may seem like a lot to learn, but it's really not difficult and the answers are all in the book.

1 ...at least two items (other than clothing) that are useful to bring on board?

2 ...how to use a gas stove safely, and why is it so important?

3 ...what is a companionway?

4 ...when you might need a safety harness and how to use one?

5 ...the difference between a sloop and a yawl?

6 ...what a sail tie is used for?

7 ...what is the purpose of the topping lift?

8 ...what part of a sail is the luff?

9 ...how a roller furling headsail works?

10 ...what part of a boat is the coachroof?

11 ...how to coil a line and how to throw one?

12 ...how to catch a turn?

13 ...how to tie a bowline and a clove hitch?

14 ...how to fold a mainsail cover correctly?

15 ...what to do with fenders when you leave harbour?

16 ...the difference between running and reaching?

17 ...when a boat is said to be 'on the wind'?

18 ...the difference between tacking and gybing?

19 ...what is meant by 'tailing' a winch?

20 ...what a riding turn is and what to do about it?

21 ...what is meant by easing sheets?

22 ...when a boat might fly a spinnaker?

23 ...what 'ready about' signifies?

24 ...what this is?

25 ...what a preventer is?

26 ...what you do with the main sheet when the boat gybes?

27 ...what happens when the boat is reefed?

28 ...what is meant by 'pinching'?

29 ...what the 'Rule of the Road' is?

30 ...what an autopilot does?

31 ...and one important thing you must know about it?

32 ...what do spring lines prevent when you are alongside?

33 ...what is meant by 'port side to'?

34 ...how to put a mooring line on a cleat when there is a line there already?

35 ...why halyards need to be well secured in harbour?

36 ...at least three things that need attention when the crew finally leave the boat?

37 ...why the anchor cable must be paid out gradually when the anchor is let go?

38 ...one way of telling if your anchor is holding?

39 ...when an anchor is said to be 'aweigh'?

40 ...what particular item must always be in the dinghy?

41 ...why you need to know what the tide is doing when you take a dinghy ashore?

42 ...where you can get a weather forecast when you go ashore?

43 ...what it means when a barometer starts to fall?

44 ...whether force 8 is good news or bad news?

45 ...what the tide is doing when it is ebbing?

46 ...how you can often use your eyes to tell what the tidal stream is doing?

47 ...what a sounding is?

48 ...how distance is measured at sea?

49 ...what this type of buoy is called?

50 ...what are the two nautical meanings of 'log'?

Glossary

Most of the words in this glossary have appeared in the text, but there are other useful nautical words that you may come across sooner or later.

NOTE: The common nautical direcyions – port, starboard, fore and aft etc are illustrated on p.16 and are not included in this glossary.

Almanac: annual publication (various types) giving details of tides, lights, harbours and other useful information.

Anchor buoy: a small buoy, sometimes used to mark the position of the anchor.

Anchor light: all round white light either hoisted on the forestay or at the masthead when at anchor.

Awash: just level with the water surface, eg a rock that just shows.

Backstay: a stay leading from the masthead to the stern.

Batten: strip of wood or plastic inserted in the *leech* of the mainsail to keep the sail's shape when it is hoisted.

Batten pocket: pocket sewn into the sail to take a *batten*.

Beacon: an unlighted navigation mark on shore or in shallow water.

Beam: a boat's breadth.

Bear away: to alter course away from the direction of the wind.

Beaufort scale: scale measuring the force of the wind, eg force 4.

Bend: type of knot for joining ropes. To 'bend on': prepare a sail for hoisting.

Berth: space for sleeping on board. Also a place where a boat can lie. (To give something a 'wide berth' means keeping well clear of it.)

Bight: a loop in a rope.

Bilges: area at the bottom of the inside of a boat, under the cabin sole.

Binnacle: housing in which the steering compass is mounted.

Block: pulley, used to be made of wood, now plastic with metal fittings.

Bollard: short squat post on a dock for taking a vessel's lines.

Boom: spar supporting the foot of a sail.

Boot top: narrow strip of paint between the bottom and the side of the hull.

Bottlescrew: (rigging screw) fitting at the foot of *shrouds* and *stays* or on a *lifeline* to adjust the tension.

Bowline: the knot for tying an eye in the end of a line.

Break out: 'breaking out' an anchor means getting it clear of the sea bed.

Broad reach: the point of sailing with the wind on the beam or just aft of the beam.

Bulkhead: a vertical partition below decks.

Burgee: triangular flag, usually representing a club, and flown at the masthead or *spreader*.

Cabin sole: the cabin deck, also the *cockpit* sole.

Chain locker: locker where the anchor chain or line is stowed.

Chainplate: fitting, firmly secured to the hull, to which shrouds are attached.

Chandler: store selling clothing, equipment, etc for sailors.

Cleat: deck fitting with two arms to which a line is secured.

Clew: the rear, lower corner of a sail to which the *sheets* are attached.

Close hauled: when a boat is sailing and heading as close to the direction of the wind as possible.

Coachroof: the top of the cabin raised above the deck.

Coaming: raised structure around openings, eg 'cockpit coaming'.

Cockpit: sunken area at the aft end of the deck where the crew sit.

Companionway: the ladder leading up to the deck from the cabin.

Course: the direction a boat is steered.

Courtesy flag: the maritime national flag of the country being visited, and flown at the starboard spreader.

CQR anchor: commonly used type of anchor, sometimes known as a 'plough' anchor because of its shape.

Cringle: a metal eye set into a sail.

Cutter: single masted sailing boat carrying two headsails.

Deck log: a book, usually kept on the chart table, in which yacht's navigation details are recorded.

Depth log: same as *echo sounder*.

Dodger: a screen for protection against the weather, fitted either side of the cockit and also showing the boat's name. Also portable shelter fitted over the companionway.

Double up: to put out extra mooring lines.

Downwind: away from the direction of the wind.

Drag: an anchor is dragging when it has not dug in and is not holding.

Draught: the distance between the bottom of the keel and the waterline.

Ease out: pay out a line slowly.

Ebb: the tide is ebbing when the water level is falling.

Echo sounder: an electronic instrument for measuring the depth of water.

Fairlead: a deck fitting giving a 'fair lead' to eg a mooring line.

Fender: a bumper, usually of air-filled plastic, used to protect a boat's hull when lying alongside a dock or another vessel.

Flood: the tide is flooding when the water level is rising.

Foot: the lower edge of a sail.

Foredeck: the deck forward of the mast.

Forestay: the supporting shroud running from the the bows to the masthead.

Foul anchor: an anchor that has caught an obstruction on the bottom.

Frap: tying halyards so that they do not slap against the mast.

Freeboard: the distance between the waterline and the deck level.

Furl: roll up or gather up a sail and tie it.

Genoa: a large headsail whose aft end overlaps the mast.

Go about: see *tack*.

Gooseneck: fitting which attaches a boom to the mast.

GPS Global Positioning System – an electronic navigation system based on information received from satellites.

Ground tackle: collective term for a boat's anchors and cables.

Gunwale (pronounced *gunnel*): top edge of the side of a boat.

Gybe: alter course from one tack to another by putting the stern through the wind.

Halyard: line used to hoist a sail.
Harden in: to haul in a sheet, eg 'harden in the main'.
Head: the top corner of a sail.
Head/heads: boat's lavatory.
Headsail: sail forward of the mast set on the forestay.

Jib: small headsail.

Ketch: two-masted sailing vessel. The main mast is the taller of the two, and the mizzen mast is forward of the rudder or steering gear.
Kicking strap: a tackle led from the foot of the mast designed to prevent the boom from lifting.
Knot: unit of speed at sea. A knot is one nautical mile per hour.

Lanyard: a short piece of small line for securing something like a sailor's knife.
Lead line (pronounced *led*): a marked line with a weight on the end, used to measure the depth of water (useful if the echo sounder breaks down).
Lee: the side away from the wind.
Leeboard: a wooden or canvas fitting on the open side of a bunk to stop you falling out.
Leech: the rear edge of a sail.
Leeward: downwind.
Lubber line: marker on a steering compass lined up with the yacht's fore and aft line.

Make fast: secure a line to a cleat or bollard.
Mast step: where the foot (*heel*) of the mast fits.
Masthead light: white light at or near the masthead used by a yacht when under power at night.

Mizzen mast: the aft mast in a yawl or ketch.
Neap tide: tide where the rise and fall is least and the stream weakest (when the moon is waning).
Navel pipe: opening in the deck leading down to the cable locker.

Painter: line used for securing the bow of a dinghy.
Pay out: to let out a rope or line without letting it go.
Pinch: sailing too close to the wind.
Plough anchor: type of anchor shaped like a ploughshare, eg CQR.
Port hand: on the port side of a boat eg a port hand buoy.
Pulpit: metal frame at the bows to which the lifelines are attached.
Pushpit: the name for the stern pulpit.

Quarter: that part of the boat between the beam and the stern, hence 'port quarter' and 'starb'd quarter'.

Reach: point of sailing with the wind on the beam or near it.
Ready about: the helmsman's warning that he is going to tack.
Reef: to reduce the area of the sails.
Riding turn: situation on a winch when one turn jams over another.
Rigging: the collective term for all the ropes and wires used to support the mast and handle the sails.
Rowlock: dinghy fitting for holding an oar.
Rubbing strake: a projecting band round the hull (yacht or dinghy) to protect it when lying alongside.
Run: point of sail with the wind from astern.
Running rigging: rigging that moves (e g halyards) as opposed to *standing rigging*.

Sail ties: strips of material used to lash a sail when it is lowered.

Scupper: a drain hole in the edge of the deck.

Seacock: a manual valve in the hull controlling the flow of water in or out.

Set: to hoist a sail.

Shackle: metal fitting with a pin for connecting rigging and chain.

Sheave: grooved wheel inside a block, to take rope or wire.

Sheet: line for controlling a sail.

Sheet in: to pull in on a sheet.

Shrouds: *standing rigging* that supports the mast on either side.

Slab reef: system of mainsail reefing.

Slack off: to ease off a line.

Slack water: period around low water and high water when there is little movement of the tide.

Sloop: single masted sailing vessel carrying a single headsdail.

Snap shackle: a shackle closed by a spring plunger and without a separate pin.

Sole: the floor of the cabin or cockpit.

Sounding: the depth of water in any place as marked on a chart .

Spinnaker: large, light, full bellied sail, flown when wind is astern.

Spreaders: struts on either side of the mast to spread the load of the *shrouds*.

Spring tide: tide where the rise and fall is greatest and the stream is strongest (around a full and new moon).

Standing rigging: mast support wires.

Stanchion: upright metal support for the lifelines fixed around the deck.

Stay: a supporting wire for the mast.

Stern gland: the opening where the propeller shaft passes through the hull.

Stern light: white light shown at the stern.

Stern line: line from the stern to the shore when mooring alongside.

Tack: (1) to alter course with the bow passing through the wind.
(2) The lower forward corner of a sail.

Take in: properly, to lower a sail, but also used to mean *sheet in*.

Tackle: combination of two blocks and a rope to provide a more powerful pull.

Telltales: strands of fine material attached to the *shrouds* or the *luffs* of headsails to indicate the apparent wind direction.

Thwart: a seat in a small boat at right angles to a line from bow to stern.

Toerail: low strip of wood or metal that runs round the edge of the deck.

Topping lift: the line from the masthead to the end of the boom, which supports it when the sail is not hoisted.

Topsides: the visible sides of a boat between the deck and the waterline.

Traveller: sliding fitting on a track, to take either the main sheet or an adjustable block for a headsail sheet.

Veer: (1) to pay out a line or cable gradually.
(2) The wind is said to veer when it changes direction clockwise.

Warp: alternative name for mooring line, also 'anchor warp'.

Weatherboards (or washboards): movable boards fitted in the companionway in bad weather.

Whipping: twine bound round the end of a rope to prevent fraying. There are various types of whipping.

Windlass: winch used for weighing anchor. May be manual or electric.

Windward: the direction from which the wind blows.

Yawl: a two-masted yacht, where the mizzen mast is aft of the rudder head.

Index